ONLY DEAD FISH GO WITH THE FLOW

THE FLOW

by Pauline Messenger

Published in 2019 by FeedARead.com Publishing

Copyright © Pauline Messenger

A CIP catalogue record for this title is available from the British
Library.

REVIEWS

The writer is very honest and she bares her soul. I liked the little anecdotes and quirky bits throughout. I welcomed some of the 'spooky' little messages sent kindly to help the reader back on their journey. A beautiful book that has everything, shame, shock, sadness, yes I even shed a tear or two. Pauline has strength! She put into words how a mother's love is tucked deep within her heart forever. Her beautiful boys have a treasure for a mum. Pauline Messenger is natural, soft and an honest person who is not afraid to share her life, beliefs and with humour to one and all.

Maureen Gillespie

I've really enjoyed reading this book, it's heartbreaking in places and had me in tears a number of times. Throughout the sadness I loved the little glimpses of humour and positivity. What a strong lady she is! Looking forward to reading 'The Misfit.'

Lesley Baker Padden

I could not put the book down, which was good for me. What an amazing journey the writer took me on and an emotional rollercoaster. I actually thought I was with her all of the way through. Totally inspirational and I now have a total new outlook on life. The writer is truly an amazing woman, an inspiration and proof that life does go on no matter what life throws at you.

Amanda Gale

An emotional journey of life's continuous struggles with love and loss are beautifully portrayed throughout this book. Pauline's faith in God during times of great hardship and grief reveals how staying connected can bring comfort during those challenging times in our lives. There are many signs and messages we often ignore that can lead us out of the darkness and this journey is evidence on just how you can do that, stay the course and follow your mission. Don't be a dead fish and go with the flow…..follow your heart and let God guide you to your inner peace that's one thing you'll certainly uncover when you read this book.

Janet Melody

It felt like I was reading a patchwork quilt filled with different squares, colours, textures, temperatures and episodes. Some were uplifting, some testing, lots funny and several sad patches. Some, all of them at the same time!

Shades of the author's life, which I am sure the readers will identify with and perhaps find themselves nodding along too. A bit of an emotional roller coaster. The tone was light at first and steadily grew to be more determined as it approached August 2016, when it took a turn down a dark road. Pauline's tenacity is remarkable, as she is herself and her story is a special one.

Peter Ellison

I sat all day and read the book from cover to cover…… couldn't put it down!!! I thoroughly enjoyed the book and am I so pleased that her faith has managed to help her get to a better place. She was so brave putting all of this on paper. She hasn't had the easiest of lives. Her son Steven sounds a character, loved by so many and of this Pauline must be so, so proud. I look forward to reading her next book 'The Misfit.'

Chris Carney

FORWARD

Suddenly I just knew, it was time to tell my story, The pen started to flow and I knew it was the start of literally a new chapter. I could feel the magic and excitement......a new beginning!

Throughout my book I have been totally honest, bared my soul and I have left nothing out. This is my story, of my journey through change, challenges, divorce, bereavement and lots more.

I hope you, my reader, not only enjoy but will get encouragement from this book, to believe in yourself knowing that whatever life throws at you, there is always light at the end of the tunnel and life really does carry on. It stops for no-one. In life we have to go through the darkness to appreciate and be grateful for the light.

A fish will persevere up stream regardless of what it has to endure and the only time it gives up is when it has died. May we take a lesson out of it's book.

ACKNOWLEDGEMENTS

I would like to thank my very dear friends Jan and Jeff Wheeler and Maria Wylie for not only your valued friendship but for your constant support throughout my darkest hours.

A huge thank you to Margaret Frankie who came immediately I rang her on 6th August 2016 and who made sure I was on the flight to Dubai by lunchtime that day and not only that she was there waiting for me on my return.

I would also like to thank my friends from the East Herrington W.I. for their friendship and fun. They made me realise just what a 'girlie' night / weekend / holiday was all about!

To Roy and Gill Spragg, Marion Walker, Anne Henderson, Jeanette Allinson and Joanne Montgomery a sincere thank you for not only your friendship but for being there to walk Alfie, get my shopping, take me for hospital appointments and for literally getting me through 2016. I couldn't have done it without you.

A special thank you to Marian Walker and Wayne Fox for the memorable C.D. of Steven's music which still helps me to get through dark moments.

Thank you to my friends and old neighbours Janet Melody and Susan Wood who have been my therapists, whether it be a coffee in Costa, a session of Reiki from Janet or Sue treating me with her homeopathic remedies….I'd truly recommend them to anyone.

A special thank you goes to Janet Melody for designing my book cover.

I will be forever in debt to Hassan, Shabs and all of the members of the Warpigs and Black Eagles (Harley Davidson families) in Dubai and of course not forgetting Chris Topher for the superb presentation of Steven's life. Your support has been unbelievable and no words of thanks can ever be enough for what you did for all of us. I am eternally grateful to all of you, for keeping Steven's memory alive. Thank you from the bottom of my heart.

A huge thank you goes to my son Paul, for his love and continuous support. Paul you have been my rock throughout all of the trauma which we have both endured. You give your mam the determination to go forward, to be the person I am meant to be and I hope I make you as proud of me, as I am of you. We have both travelled this journey together and if it is at all possible, it has deepened our love for each other and strengthened the unbreakable bond which is between a mother and her son. You truly are the light of my life.

I am forever grateful to my parents. My dad passed on his great wisdom and taught me lessons which have helped me throughout my life. Whilst my mum gave me determination to succeed no matter what life throws at me. Mum I understand you so much more now and also realise how much pain you endured.

I would like to thank Lynn Davidson of The Memoir Club for guiding me to the finishing post.

And finally I would like to thank my ex husband because without his actions, I would not be the

8

independent, strong woman I am today. God bless you for giving me my beautiful boys, Steven and Paul.

INTRODUCTION

Everyone has a story, I read this in a book and it was my lifetime ambition, to write my story.

At the beginning of 2016, I came down with a bout of viral pneumonia and whilst I was recovering, words started to come into my head. I wrote them down and by the July I had written a book.

However, in August that year, I went through what is every parent's nightmare, I lost my beautiful 29 year old son, Steven. I felt I wanted to write and share with you what I went through over the next few months.

This book is how, through events in my life, I was able to 'Turn My Life Around.' I hope it helps you to. It is about darkness and light and every shade in-between.

CONTENTS

You Never Know How Strong You Are Until Being Strong Is The Only Choice You Have.

Wow! This is a big one and don't I know it. I have been tested quite a few times in my life but I think by far one of the worst times was when my life changed big time! Was I ready for what was to come? No way!

But first I will go back to when I left my job on 31st October 1986, after working for sixteen years with Midland Bank, to start my maternity leave. I had worked there from leaving school, at the age of sixteen.

I had six wonderful years bringing up my little boy Steven, who was born on 11 December 1986. It was one of the things I had so wanted to be in life, a mum.

Then in April 1991, my husband said he didn't want to be in the business he was in anymore. I had persuaded him to buy a milk round in 1974, when his dad had had a massive stroke and I had thought that this was one way that he could be at home to help his mum and still work.

All of my family were in the milk business and so when he bought his milk business, my dad had helped him to get the business up and running and I had done the bookwork for him. So back to 1991, after some discussion, he said he wanted to be out of the business by the time he was forty. In other words now! So I said okay, put the business up for sale, which he did and it was sold within a week.

We went a year without him working, our savings were being used up but we tried to stay positive. We looked at wine bars, pubs and hotels. His family had been in the licence trade and he himself had been a night club manager when I had first started going out with him. So our search continued.

There was one hotel in particular which we had put an offer in for but the offer kept getting rejected. I said we had to stick to our guns, that was what we could afford and if it was meant to be, we would get it.

In May 1992, we bought our hotel. We worked seventeen hours a day, seven days a week. Not only was I trying to run a business with my husband but I was bringing up our son, trying to run a separate home and I had for the first two years, our mums staying overnight. My mum stayed four nights each week and his mum stayed three.

Both mums had been widowed early in life, so they welcomed the company. I also had to prepare meals for everyone. I had Steven's homework to oversee and after school activities to attend, as neither of the mums could drive and Steven's school was two miles away. I would see to everything after we had closed the bar and carvery at 3:00 p.m on an afternoon.

In 1992 licence premises closed between 3:00 p.m. and 6:00 p.m. We would pick Steven up from school and whichever mum was on duty that night. We would go home, hubby would go to bed for a sleep and I would do what I had to do then get washed and changed after tea and be ready to go back to work for 6 p.m. when we re-opened.

Meanwhile our receptionist held the fort, so to speak, whilst we were off the premises, overseeing anyone checking in to the hotel.

December 1993, I realised I was pregnant, how was I going to cope? Working the hours I was but more importantly how was I going to deal with the Morning Sickness because I was not only sick as soon as I got up on a morning, no, I was sick all day and it was the last thing I did before I went to bed at night. I was finding life really difficult, trying to work at the hotel and also run the family home.

The first time I saw the gynaecologist he sat and told me how the risks had gone up from when I was pregnant at 32 to being pregnant at 39. He asked for my permission to do three blood tests which were needed to check that the baby was okay. He also asked me to have a think about what I would want to do if the blood test results came back positive, showing that there was something wrong with the baby.

It didn't take much thinking, I thought this baby is a gift from God and no way would I want to get rid of it. When I went back to see the consultant, I told him my decision and he said it was alright because all of the tests had come back clear.

I was feeling so ill that I suggested taking the office home which would enable me to work in the study, when I was feeling up to it. At the same time my hubby suggested we promote the bar manageress/receptionist to assistant manageress, to ease his load and he also suggested that we give her a set of keys for the office and the safe. This we did.

16

I visited my consultant on the 24th August 1994, they were keeping a close eye on me. I must admit it had never even entered my head before I was pregnant that pregnancy was so much more dangerous as you got older.

The, what the consultant described as niggles, at 11 a.m. that morning became full blown contractions by 9 p.m. that night. I had been too busy sitting, catching up on paperwork and getting accounts ready for the accountant, to notice that I was having contractions regularly.

Suddenly I had a strong contraction and I thought I must jot down the time of when I had had it. I then realised that my contractions were coming every seven minutes. I thought I had better phone hubby and tell him to not stay back after work and could he please pick my mum up on the way, which he did, as we would need someone to mind Steven for us, whilst we went to the hospital.

I continued to work until 12:30 a.m. I had a bowl of cereal before I decided it was time to go. When I had had Steven I went two days without food, as he took his time making his entry into this world and I didn't want to be caught out again.

I had phoned the hospital at 11 p.m. to tell them that I would be going in and to expect me. However by the time I finished my jobs and made my way there, waddling to the ward, the staff had given up on me, saying they had thought that it had all just been a false alarm.

Well at 3 a.m. I had the most excruciating pain and I was told the baby's heart rate had dropped drastically. I was given an epidural and the midwife monitored me.

These piercing pains occurred five more times over the next few hours and on the fifth, the consultant was called for. He explained that my gynaecologist liked his babies to arrive wearing their school uniform but he said that he wanted the baby out and he wanted it out now. I was rushed to theatre for an emergency 'C' section, saying if I was going to theatre, then hubby was coming with me. On the 25th August 1994, at 11:15 a.m. I gave birth to the most beautiful baby boy, Paul James, who is the light of my life.

After a few days, once we were home from a five day hospital stay, I found my hubby to be finding every excuse in the book to spend most of his time at the hotel. Meanwhile I, recovering from my 'C' section, was finding it very hard to try and look after my new baby, see to Steven and also look after the house and the bookwork for the hotel.

It was all getting too much for me, I was not coping very well and I started to feel unwell. So much so, that by the time Paul was five weeks old I felt so ill, I rang for a home visit from my G.P.

The doctor actually visited on the Thursday then a different G.P. visited me on the Saturday after I had requested a further visit.

I was so ill, that the doctor who came out on the Saturday morning, rang me at 10 p.m. on the Saturday evening to see if I was feeling any better and I told him I was no better. The next morning, Sunday, the doctor just happened to be passing by and thought he would pop in to see me.

He told me I was lying in the bed half dead, his words, not mine. He whipped me into hospital. He had to find a side ward for me, as I had to take Paul with me because I was breast feeding.

Once I was settled in the side ward I was given antibiotics intravenously. I was found to be suffering from a womb infection, a kidney infection and mastitis. No wonder I felt so ill.

Visiting time hubby came in, with Steven plus the homework for me to oversee. He was wondering what he would do if I wasn't out by the Thursday, when the wages for our forty employees needed to be done.

Looking back now I realise that after I came out of the hospital, I started to go downhill and in hindsight I had also had post natal depression.

My sister Joy, would come after tea each night and ask what she could do to help me. It was like being a single mum, hubby was nowhere to be seen, he just came home to sleep and that was normally around 3:00-3:30 a.m. the next morning.

From 1997-2000, I found I was having numerous rows with my hubby, I was saying that there was money going missing from the hotel. There was a discrepancy in the accounts. I just couldn't pinpoint where the money was going from. Hubby more or less blamed it on me, saying I was being negligent.

Then on June 11th 2000, he found out that our assistant manageress was stealing from a wedding party we were catering for. My suspicions had been confirmed because hubby had found her stealing from a customer and not from ourselves, he felt the need to inform the police.

On visiting the assistant manageress at her parents' home, where she lived and after searching her bedroom, the police found fifty eight thousand pounds in cash, stuffed in shoe boxes and carrier bags under her bed.

We had a visit from the police informing us of their findings and that night I stayed up all night and went through a year's bookwork recording every shortage we had had over the year, to see just where she was stealing the money from.

Yes, we had unexplainable big losses over the last few years, from the safe and tills and after several rows hubby had given in and asked her to hand over her keys.

Unfortunately the two of us had had a huge row a few days later. The reason for the row was that he told me he was going to give the keys back to her.

We had twelve tills in the hotel, she had access to all of them. Even the tin with the waitress tips went missing. She also had access to the daily takings in the safe. So once hubby had cashed up, she had access to the takings before I went in on a Friday to do the wages.

During the time up until the case went to court, I had to deal with hubby along with our solicitor being arrested for Perverting the Cause of Justice. Hubby had unknowingly to the police and myself, arranged to meet her to try and make a deal.

The police, once hubby had confessed to them that he had had a five year affair with her, thought that they were both stealing from me.

The Friday before the case was due to be heard at Crown Court, we were told that the barrister who was acting on our behalf was withdrawing from the case. They were going to cancel the case altogether meaning the case could not go ahead. We were shocked and we insisted that the case had to go to court, they would have to find a new barrister to represent us.

A barrister who did not know anything about the case or the past three years it had been going on for, came up from Bradford to represent us and fight our case.

The detectives had also told hubby that he had to inform me of the affair he had been having with the assistant manageress for the past five years and if he didn't, then they would inform me. They gave him three days to do so.

He woke me up at 2:45 a.m. on the Friday morning to tell me. Afterwards I silently got out of bed and made my way downstairs. I felt numb inside, I could not say a thing. I spent the rest of the night in the lounge, sitting in the armchair, trying to get my head around what I had been told, which I had always suspected but which he had firmly denied. I had to decide what to do.

By the time daylight dawned, I had decided I would stand by him. You might think I was stupid but the reason I chose to do so was that it would not look good in court if we were not speaking and so I decided we would be a united front, so to speak.

However I did say that if I ever found out that he was cheating on me again, then that would be us finished.

We spent three harrowing years dealing with the court case against our assistant manageress and eventually on the second day at Crown Court she pleaded guilty to stealing fifty thousand pounds.

Later, after the case had been adjourned for sentencing, the barrister having not had the time to understand the intricate details about the case, wrote to the judge and asked if we could have interest on the fifty thousand pounds.

The judge on the day of sentencing agreed to us being rewarded interest on the money due to the time it had taken to be heard in court and so we received eight thousand pounds interest.

In other words we were awarded the full amount which the police had recovered from her home. She was given a nine month jail sentence, of which she actually served two and a half months.

She went to jail and we tried to get on with our lives. It had hit every daily newspaper and everyone wanted to know just what had been going on. It was very difficult and our marriage was very frail.

Eighteen months later I found out that he was seeing a nineteen year old girl. He was fifty four at the time, old enough to be her grandfather. I told him I wanted a divorce. He didn't seem to understand what I was saying and said yes he knew we needed to talk but not get a divorce.

I worked in the hotel until I could no longer cope with the verbal abuse. It was so bad that one day I was forced to phone my solicitor and ask if I could just walk out and would it be okay to take enough money from our account to live on. He said of course it was. I wasn't sure what he would do with the hotel but my mental state of health was more important. I was also experiencing acute angina.

Hubby, over the next year was so verbally abusive towards me. He wouldn't get out of the family home, threatening me that if I locked him out, he would smash the windows.

I was sleeping, with my solicitor's advice, locked in my bedroom for my safety. Hubby would put a clothes horse, in front of my bedroom door, full of shirts hanging on it, to try and block my exit.

One night when I was having a severe angina attack and had to call 999, the paramedics found it difficult to get in to me. Once they were in my bedroom, hubby appeared and stood in the doorway, not saying a word and at the same time blocking their exit. My neighbour and good friend Maria had come in to pack an overnight bag for me.

I had to wait until I was in the ambulance before I felt safe enough to inform the ambulance men of what was going on.

Another night I approached hubby with regards to closing the joint account, I was paying all of the home bills and he was not contributing towards any of them. He had tight hold of my wrists, then my arms and when Paul came downstairs to ask what all the shouting was about, he let go and took Paul upstairs. I followed behind and unknown to Paul, his dad was kicking me and trying to push me down the stairs.

I was now training to be an holistic therapist therefore the next day when I went in to college, one of my colleagues noticed the bruising. She knew that the bruising had not been there the day before and advised me to phone my solicitor, which I did. Then the solicitor told me to go to my G.P. The G.P. advised me to go to my local police station and report it. So I went to the police station after seeing the doctor.

The policeman filed a report and once I had told him everything that had been going on, he informed me that the mental abuse I had been the victim of was actually worse than the physical abuse. He asked me to go to the main police station to enable them to photograph the bruising.

The police rang me on the Saturday evening to ask me if I knew where my husband was and I told them that he was at work. They informed me that no he wasn't because they had arrested him and were keeping him in custody.

At 7 a.m. on the Sunday morning, they released him, phoning me to apologise and to warn me that he was on his way home. I locked my bedroom door and stayed inside until he had arrived back and I couldn't hear him moving about.

Several days later my keys went missing and a friend advised me to call the locksmith out that evening and have the lock changed on my bedroom door. This I did and whilst the locksmith was there, we could hear someone on the other side of the door trying to kick the door down.

I rang the police. The locksmith stayed with me and said he would give them a statement and be a witness. When the police arrived they noticed the photographs which had been taken of the bruising, lying on my bed. They wanted to know who was responsible for the bruising? When I told them it was my husband who was downstairs, they told me that they couldn't leave me in the house, as my life was in danger.

And so at 12:45 a.m. the police asked me to ring my sister to see if I could go and stay with her. Earlier that evening I had asked Paul to go to his Auntie Joy's. She lived in the same street as we did. I had had a feeling of dread, I just knew something awful was going to happen.

I had to stay at my sister's home for three weeks whilst Paul stayed at my niece's home. She had a young son who Paul got on really well with and we thought it would take his mind off what was happening.

There was one week when I had to go in front of the judge daily, as each day I was experiencing threatening behaviour towards me. On the fourth day, the judge told me my life was in danger.

The case eventually came before the judge, in the family court. After hearing both sides, the judge adjourned for thirty five minutes. When she summed up the case, she gave my husband one week to move out of the family home. He took Steven with him, as he had told Steven that although he had had the affair, I was splitting the family up, it was all my fault. They moved into rented accommodation.

Eventually on 17th December 2005 Paul and I were allowed to move back into the family home.

Over the next few months I would wake up and find six inch nails in my car tyres. One night when the hubby was dropping Paul off, he stood on my drive shouting "I wish you would die!"

Paul broke down and cried. My friend was sitting in the lounge and she could hear what was going on. She helped me to console Paul.

Three times in one week I was admitted to A & E and when I was admitted the third time, I thought they needed to know just what I was going through to enable them to help me. The house doctor talked to me for an hour and a half, she promised me that they would help me get through this mess and I have to say they kept their word. In fact my health deteriorated so much that I eventually had to have a stent fitted.

My husband wanted to put the business into liquidation then he tried to bankrupt us. He said if he couldn't have the business then no way was I getting anything.

I received a phone call one Monday afternoon, the following July, it was the bailiff, he was at the hotel. He said that there was thirty eight thousand pounds owing to the Customs and Excise and I jointly owned the business, so therefore I was jointly liable. He told me he was coming to see me. Unknown to me, when I walked out of the hotel my husband stopped paying any bills.

I rang my solicitor, I just did not know what to do, it was emotional blackmail. He told me to shut the blinds and go out and stay out, which I did. On my return at teatime, there was a note on the doormat saying the bailiff had been and he was coming back.

By this time the solicitor's office was closed for the day and so I rang a friend, who was a solicitor and she told me to clear everything out of the house. When I say everything, I mean everything.

Jan, my very dear friend, who lives in the U.S.A. was actually home, in the U.K., she has a house on the same estate where I lived. I rang her and she said that she and Jeff, her husband would come up. Jeff drove my car away and Maria, Noel, (Maria's husband) and Jan helped me to clear the house. Two of my nephews came with their vans and took some of my furniture to Jan's to be stored in her garage, the rest was stored in Maria and Noel's garage.

It took us one and a half hours to clear a big four bedroom detached house. Whilst we were busy emptying it, I walked along the hallway and there stood in the open doorway, was the bailiff. I panicked, fortunately Maria, Noel and Jan were in Maria's house, the double doors to my lounge were standing wide open. The bailiff could see that the lounge was stripped bare, not even a picture was left on the wall nor the T.V. standing.

I told him that my husband was using emotional blackmail and that there was enough money to pay the bills, would he please get in touch with my solicitor. He told me that there was so much collateral, he would give me twenty four hours.

After he left, we continued emptying the house, until there was only two beds, one chair and enough cutlery and crockery for Paul and I.

That night I put Paul to bed and every time he tried to shut his eyes he started screaming. By 11 p.m. I phoned Jan, I was in despair, I just didn't know what to do. She told me to take Paul to her house and for the two of us to stay with her, which we did for four nights until it was time for Jan and Jeff to return to the States by which time we returned home.

On the Saturday, after we returned home, something inside of me snapped, I couldn't cope any longer. I think I cried for three hours. Paul cried with me, we stood in each other's arms and cried our hearts out. I made him a promise that day. I said I promised him that we would get through this mess.

When the crying eventually subsided, I told myself "Come on girl, have a bath, wash your hair, put your make up on and show the world what you are made of!"

I was supposed to be having friends around for supper that evening, I didn't cancel. I asked Maria if I could borrow her garden furniture and we put it all into my lounge and I entertained my friends.

I thought if they were true friends then they would accept me for who I am and if not, then they weren't worth having.

Someone brought a dessert and I apologised, informing them that I only had two spoons and two bowls. They said that we were all friends together and if we couldn't share a bowl then it was a bad job.

It was one of the biggest lessons of my life, humility!

Two weeks later I had gone out with my mum for the day, Paul was at school and I just needed a break. I had thirty two telephone calls from my accountant that day, who between the two of us were trying to sort out this mess. The bailiff had sent a removal truck which was apparently in the hotel car park ready to empty the hotel.

The accountant, acting on my behalf, just happened to mention that my husband hadn't even been in touch with his solicitor. He was doing nothing and so I told my accountant to just let it all go, if he wasn't bothered then why should I be? I called his bluff and what do you know, he produced a cheque just before they started to empty the hotel.

I received a text from Paul that day to say,

"Dad says you can put your furniture back!"

Now if that is not emotional blackmail then what is?

Never let money rule you, it is not worth it.

I went away a few weeks later, on my own, in a cottage, in the country. Paul was spending time with his dad. I spent my days meditating and praying and spent a lot of time talking to God. I asked for a buyer for the hotel and could we get the price it was worth. We had worked hard over these past fourteen years to build the business up, with very few days off and having very few holidays.

I arrived home on the Thursday evening and received a phone call from a gentleman who wanted to know if I was aware that he had put an offer in for the hotel. In actual fact, unknown to me and considering we had not advertised the hotel for sale, there were five different people fighting over the hotel.

In the end we got the price which I thought the business was worth. My prayers had indeed been answered.

When I got divorced I lost my business, my job, my husband, my elder son for a while, I wasn't sure if I would loose my home and my husband had told lies to my family and so now they weren't speaking to me. He had told them that I had received all the money from the divorce settlement and he was left with nothing when in actual fact he came out of the settlement with seventy thousand pounds more than me.

I had survived to see another day, hopefully many more! I, by this time was about to qualify as an Holistic Therapist, something I had always wanted to do.

I would like to take this opportunity to say, I don't have time to hate anyone who hates me. I am too busy loving the people who love me.

I am also very grateful and thankful to everyone in my past because without them I wouldn't be the person I am today.

I am lead to understand that Steven and his dad had had an argument and his dad had called the police. The police actually rang me and asked if Steven could come to me. Then Steven came on the phone and said "Mum can I come back home? I can't live with dad anymore." I told him that it was my home now and my rules and just like the prodigal son he returned home to live with Paul and myself.

Christmas 2013 saw Steven in a quandary, I had moved to the country whilst he was touring California on his Harley Davidson and before he went he said, what was he going to do over Christmas, as on January 1st 2014 he was starting a new job in Dubai, working for Harley Davidson. I had moved twenty six miles away from his dad, to the country. Steven wanted to see both of us. So I suggested that he invite his dad for Christmas. It was ten years since the divorce and during that time I had done a lot of work on releasing and forgiving the past.

We stayed under one roof, my roof, for eight days, without a cross word. All was calm and peaceful, the ex even washed the dishes, something he had never done in the past.

I did have to laugh, when, standing with his arms crossed, watching me put curtains up he said "I don't know how you have managed without me for all this time?"

"Very well!" I thought with a smile.

Forgiveness

Through the following days, months, years I worked through all of my heartache and pain. It had been a very dark, deep hole I had found myself at the bottom of and I realised that the only way was up.

At times I felt I was sliding back down but eventually as I forgave all of the tears I was made to shed, along with all the betrayal, lies, pain and disappointment, I slowly was able to go in the right direction, towards the light.

I also realised to move on I had to forgive the slanders and deceit, the hatred and persecution. I forgave the hostility, jealousy, anger and cruelty.

I lastly forgave the world and all the injustice and evil.

One day I made it to the top of that hole and what a good place it was.

When we can forgive ourselves and others, it enables us to move on with our lives.

Do You Ever Wonder Why You Are Here On Earth?

Some people know what their gifts / passions are from a very early age. I believe it is when you are doing what you love best and feel happiest doing.

As I mentioned, I started my working career by working in a bank, my dad had taught me how to do his business accounts when I was just twelve years of age and it had developed into my love of working with figures.

At the same time my mum was catering for weddings, held in her brother's pub. I would help her with the preparations the night before the wedding, then I 'waitered on' at the weddings, earning myself a little bit pocket money.

I worked in Binns Department Store, in the Dissection Office, as a Saturday girl before eventually starting work at sixteen, in our local Midland Bank. I worked for sixteen years and got as far as I could up the ladder before I left. In those days women were not allowed to take bankers exams.

I left work on October 31st 1986, to have my elder son, Steven and because I had waited a long time for him to come along, I decided I would not return to work but instead I would stay at home and enjoy his early years.

I still did my husband's business accounts, keeping my finger in the pie, so to speak and my brain active, so that I didn't go gaga with the constant playing of nursery rhymes and watching Fireman Sam.

When Steven was six, as I said previously we sold the business and whilst looking for another business we got the opportunity to go to Tenerife for a month's holiday.

We were so stressed out, we needed a break and I had won a week's holiday in Tenerife, which we asked if we could extend to a month and pay the difference, which we did. We just had to get away, de-stress then come back and continue our search.

We bought the business, the one hubby had dreamed of owning and it meant we both worked very long hours.

In lots of ways it was an exciting time, I had to set up systems, learn to use Sage programmes, do wages. We had forty staff. A huge responsibility, because if we failed, there would be forty families that would be effected. This alone gave me a grim determination to make it a success.

Yes, it was very stressful and exhausting but at the same time, exhilarating. My adrenalin would be flowing when I was in meetings with the bank manager (my old boss, I was the customer now) and the accountants. I got a real buzz from it. I could feel my brain saying "Bring it on!"

We loved catering for people's weddings, overseeing their day. I'd have a tear in my eye, as I stood listening to the speeches. I was always Toastmaster for these occasions until the week before I gave birth to my second son. I loved to see everyone leave happy, taking their happy memories with them, we knew we had done our job well.

I also, even though it sounds sad, got pleasure from catering for funerals. Looking after everyone when they came in upset, frozen and mentally exhausted. We would make sure the room was lovely and warm and we would provide a bowl of hot homemade soup for them before they had their buffet.

Yes the hours in my office were long, tedious and lonely but I enjoyed going down into the public areas and socialising with the general public and staff. I am so very much a people person.

Two years after we bought the hotel, I found out I was pregnant. I panicked, how would I cope but as they say God does not give you what you can't cope with and so I looked forward to giving birth to our second child, six months before my fortieth birthday.

I survived, don't ask me how, it was so, so hard. I grabbed five minutes sleep at every opportunity. I live to tell the tale. I worked right up until I left the house to go to the hospital as my labour pains were pretty frequent. I resumed my work, which was brought into the hospital, seven hours after I had had an emergency 'C' section.

Nine years on, we had had the business fourteen years, our marriage was on the rocks, I was exhausted, very low, my health was deteriorating and I thought if I don't do something drastic, I won't be here to look after the boys. That was what made me make the decision to file for a divorce. Paul was only nine and he needed his mum.

Whilst waiting for the divorce to be finalised, I signed up for a college course in Holistic Therapies and although it was very scary, it was quite exhilarating. I loved every single bit of the course and I actually found me.

I had walked into the college at the beginning of September that year, not as someone's daughter, sister, wife or mum but as me. I had never been in this position for a long time but I can tell you it was quite liberating.

I walked into the classroom, sat on one of the chairs in the circle and waited until it was my turn to introduce myself. A new exciting chapter was starting in my life and it certainly felt right. I felt young, light hearted, I was with younger girls, it was amazing.

It actually got me through one of the most traumatic years in my life but because we gave each other massages each day in class, as part of the course I was on, it helped to relieve the stress and helped me cope on a day to day basis.

God really does send us little miracles to help us to get through the most life changing chapters of our lives.

I was introduced to angels whilst I was on this course by a lady called Victoria who was Russian and she told me she was a white witch, which had been handed down to her from her grandmother.

This lead me months later to be given the opportunity to qualify as an Angelic Reiki Master and also become a member of the British Healers Association. I had been put on my spiritual journey.

I was able to help people wherever I went and at the same time I was there to spend quality time with my mum, who was not getting any younger, she was eighty three years of age and thirteen years previously she had undergone a quadruple heart bypass. They said it would last 10 years, she actually lived until two months before her ninety fourth birthday. I know where I get my determination from.

As mum was deteriorating, she moved in with myself and my sons until a time when I no longer could cope with nursing her, she needed proper nursing and so had to go into a nursing home. I found this one of the hardest decisions to make, as I had always told her that I would never put her into a home.

I must say that this made me realise that we must never make promises we are not sure we will be able to keep.

Mum told me one night in hospital, when she thought she was dying, to go and do what I had always wanted to do, which was to move to the country.

Mum went into the nursing home in the November and the very next day I sold my house to a first time buyer, who wanted to move in within six weeks, two weeks before Christmas 2013.

I had cared and been there for my family for all of my life. I helped people daily but I felt it was now time for me. I moved December 12th that year and I still travelled to Sunderland to see my mum every day and the last six days of her life, I stayed at her bedside 24/7, only leaving her when I had to eat, wash and go to the toilet. I was holding her hand as she past over.

I have actually been with my mum, dad and brother when they past. I would stay with a stranger, if I thought they were going to be on their own when they past over. I feel that it is a very special privilege to be with someone as they breathe their last breath.

Never be frightened, death is not frightening, our loved ones are continuing their journey, we may not see them but they are just a breath away.

I realise now, looking back on my early life, my hobbies and Saturday job, put me in good stead for what had to come. I had also been a member of an organisation, Ladies Circle, which organised fellowship events, catered for large functions and also organised fund raising events. I also had to be toastmaster in front of 500 women at a function. This all helped me when we bought the hotel. Yes I was on the right road but I do think it was all just a stepping stone to get to the next chapter.

I was honoured to be given free time, to allow me to look after my mum, as she neared the end of her life here on Earth, which was very rewarding as she had given so much of her time and devotion to me during her life.

I also found I got the opportunity to discuss things which she had done in the past which had upset me and which after some thought, mum apologised, not realising her action had hurt me and I forgave her, enabling us to put everything to rest.

I later realised that many people do not get this opportunity. I was so grateful that I had been given that time.

Another one of my gifts is to turn things around. If someone is being very negative, I can always see the positive side to it and maybe lift their moods. Some friends ring when they are low, as they say I'm like a tonic, by the time they go off the phone they are smiling and laughing.

However I did find it hard whilst I was grieving, as my friends found it difficult to accept I wasn't the usual bubbly me.

I am also very good at organising and I have a very logical brain. I'm always working out the quickest way to do things or the quickest route if I am out in my car.

What are you good at? You don't have to be an inventor, singer or actor, you could be a very good listener, which in itself, is a true gift. You may not even be aware of your gift(s) but if you ask others, I bet you that they will be able to tell you what it is that you are good at.

Love

What has happened to love?

In today's society we all seem to know what the love of money is about but we seem to have forgotten the meaning of love.

To love our bodies, this beautiful body which we were born with, not what botox and every other enhancement can do for our bodies.

Be happy with what you have, love it, take care of it, nourish it but whatever you do stop abusing it. It has to last a lifetime, so please, please, please, take care of it.

Please try and appreciate your parents, they brought you into this world after all. They have cared for you, don't you think it would be good to care about them, instead of being very focused on the self. Treat them, care for them, take time out to phone them, how much time have they devoted to you?

Instead of neglecting and humiliating our elders, respect them, take time out to visit them, take care of them. They too like to go out for meals, go to the pictures or live performances, they are still young at heart.

Parents think giving their children money to go and treat themselves is what their children want. What they do want, is for you, the parent, to take time out of your busy schedule and spend time playing with them, talking to them, baking with them, or gardening, whatever you are doing include them. Make them feel loved and part of your life.

In the future, will they remember you giving them money? The answer is no but if you have spent quality time with them making memories, they will remember that, I am sure.

We buy them all of the up to date electronic equipment but what for? For them to sit in their rooms, isolated, watching or playing with their games, enabling you to have peace and quiet, maybe a bottle of wine and a pizza and sit on your computers/mobile phones talking to friends or playing games.

Why, oh why, can't we sit as a family, around a table, sharing what each of us has done throughout the day, enjoying home cooked food which has been prepared with love. We would all feel so much better.

Get out into the real world, with your families, make real friends, enjoy each other's company.

Be proud to be who you are, value what our ancestors worked very hard for, have pride in your country. Keep traditions, this is what made us who we are.

We aren't offending other countries or other nationalities living in our country. They came here to enjoy what we have. If you are British, respect the Royal family, it is part of who you are. Other countries would love to have a Royal Family.

Every country has a faith(s) but there is a high percentage of British people who say they don't have one. What is wrong with having a faith? When we have faith, we can hope.

Please, please, please have pride in who you are, love your families and your country and with LOVE we can hopefully change the world.

The Pain Of Loving

I had been separated from my husband for two years, when I decided I would go on a dating site.

I met one or two men for coffee then there was this one, who sent me very witty messages. I wasn't fussed about his photo (he was much better in person) but I loved his quick wit and so I went along with it.

He wanted to meet up for coffee. We arranged a meeting, I was not feeling marvellous, I was full of cold and to be honest I would maybe have been better cancelling and arranging another day but I thought it's just a coffee, I am getting out of the house and it might make me feel a bit better.

On the way to where I was meeting him I got a text saying "Are you giddy, excited, nervous or just snotty?"

I arrived at the meeting place, he pulled up in his car behind me. I got out of my car, as he got out of his and when our eyes met, I was bowled over. He was most charming and I fell hook, line and sinker for him.

Unfortunately we both had excess baggage to deal with before we could commit to a long lasting relationship.

One thing I did learn was if you go internet dating, treat it as fun. Think of yourself as if you are in a supermarket, pick one off the shelf, try it and if you don't like it, put it back and choose another one.

Don't ever think, oh I don't like this about them and believe that you will be able to change them because you won't.

Also be careful, as you don't want what you have just let go of or put back on to the shelf. You don't want them to treat you mean, you deserve so much better than that. Look at it as a game and if you win, good for you and if not put it down to experience.

One other thing I will say is, you have to love yourself first. How can someone else love you if you don't love yourself. Enjoy living on your own then you know they have to be very special if you want them to be part of your life because you are content just as you are. When you know what makes you happy then you know just what you do want in your life and more importantly, what you don't want.

Remember better to have loved and lost than not to have loved at all.

Good luck with your search!

Affairs

If your partner is having an affair, do you turn a blind eye? Can you forgive and forget? Maybe if you love them so much, maybe you can.

Or do you both live in the same house but live separate lives?

Or do you divorce and either find someone else or live on your own?

I was told by someone to do the same as my husband, for both of us to have affairs and stay together but I'm sorry I couldn't live like that. I could not live a lie.

Many times after I got divorced I pondered on had I done the right thing? The answer I came up with every time was YES! I so deserved better than being controlled and having to put up with mental abuse. The lonely days and nights at first made me question as to whether or not I had indeed made the right decision.

I no longer question my decision, I have been on my own for thirteen years now and have experienced some of the most amazing adventures. I don't feel alone, I am actually content with my lot and very happy too and very grateful I have been given the time to find out who the real me is.

Divine Guidance

In hindsight, looking back over events which happened in December 2015, I truly believe our Guardian Angels were looking after us.

I was in Keswick with friends, before the adverse weather conditions and floods occurred. On the Thursday, myself and three friends had been on an outing to Ambleside. We visited the garden centre there, we just needed to be indoors as it was raining so hard. Then after we had had our lunch we decided to go to the Lakeland Store in Windermere.

The weather was not good, it had been raining very heavily all day. After looking around the Lakeland Store, we decided we would go and have a coffee and a scone in the shop's cafeteria, then head back to Keswick, to our hotel. We were attending the hotel's Christmas Party Night and wanted plenty of time to get ready.

As we made our way to the car, we noticed that the rain was now coming down heavier than ever, if that was at all possible and it had come in dark very early, obviously due to the rain. I was driving and we were heading back to The Country Manor House Hotel in Keswick, where we were on a Christmas three day break.

I drove back in torrential rain and what didn't help was, there was no lighting on the country roads, it was pitch black.

As I was driving along, I happened to notice something white out of the corner of my right eye. As I got closer, the white object became clearer, it was a gushing waterfall coming off the field, onto the main road, the one I was driving along. As we got nearer, the car started to aquaplane. I carefully drove through it and no sooner had I done so, I noticed another one in front of me. Again the car aquaplaned and I slowly and carefully manoeuvred my way forward.

At this time, my friends were expressing how grateful they were that it was me doing the driving and not them. I meanwhile was quietly praying and asking for Divine help to get us back to the hotel safely.

We did do so, I am very pleased to say and as I turned into the road where we were staying, our hotel being at the top of this road, I happened to notice that the stream running parallel to the road was very close to bursting it's banks.

I can't express how grateful I was to be walking safely into the hotel. The rest of the girls went up to their rooms and I went straight to the bar, I needed a stiff drink. I don't normally drink but I felt both physically and mentally exhausted and was in great need of one.

The next day it was on the News that the road we had been on had actually been washed away. I told the girls that morning at breakfast about our close escape and because there were Force 10 gales expected that day and we had to drive over the highest point in England, which is Alston, to get home, I decided I wanted to set off for home as soon as we had had our breakfast, which we did.

We later heard that the stream, close to our hotel, had indeed flooded it's banks and if we had been any later setting off, we would not have got home, as the hotel had been cut off.

It was teatime by the time we got back to my home in Weardale. The girls transferred their bags into their car, which had been left at mine, enabling us to all travel together. They got on their way without delay, everyone wanting to get home safely.

I set to, unpacking one case, the one with jumpers, thermals and trousers in it and started packing my larger case with summer clothes and flip flops, as I was leaving early the next morning, to travel to Dubai, to visit my sons, as they both lived there.

I woke to a power cut, the storms had brought power cables down and I had to use a torch to finish my packing. I couldn't even have a shower or wash my hair, I had no service on my mobile phone and thank goodness I had a landline which enabled me to arrange my lift to the airport.

On our way to the airport, we noticed that there were trees down and flooding on quite a number of roads but we made it. Even the Emirates aeroplane had to be brought up to the airport buildings due to the force of the wind.

I was later informed that the power cuts had lasted fifty six hours by which time I was safely in Dubai.

Was I being watched over? Without a doubt!

You Always Choose Whether To Be A Victim Or Victor Of Circumstance.

I don't know about you, my reader, but I always did feel like I was a victim of circumstance. How did I change it? I moved away, enabling me to live my own life, the way I wanted to live it!!!

I was then able to live without people trying to control me, telling me what I should or should not be doing with my life.

When we stop and think about it, it is amazing how we just 'go along' with what others want us to do.

I was in a relationship for thirty two years when I suddenly had my wake up call, I was living his dream and feeling very unhappy and my health was suffering because of it but when I stopped and said enough, yes, I had a long hard fight on my hands with people telling me that's not what I want. Excuse me!!! How do you know what I want!

I think a lot of people as they get close to their 50's, have a reality check. Is this where they want to be in the next 10-20 years? Are they happy? What is missing in their lives? Are they loved?

We are the only people who can change our lives. We can't expect others to change and comply with us. Maybe it's time for a reality check with everyone around you. It is good for you, just as it is good to clear out cupboards and old papers, to go through our relationships and move on from those which are no longer working for us or maybe they are very one sided.

Are you always the giver and they the taker. We need balance in our lives, we do deserve to be loved, to be cared for.

Is it time to be the Victor instead of the Victim? It gives us such freedom and also peace of mind. Good luck, have fun doing it, never feel guilty, this is your life, to do with, what you want. It is no good getting to the age of 80-90 and thinking I wish!!!!

Go on do it! Reclaim your freedom, take the bull by the horns and clear your life with everything which is not working. Then you will feel as if a great weight has been lifted off your shoulders, your health will improve, you will become happy in your own space because you are somewhere you want to be, with people you want in your life, doing what you enjoy.

Clear out the cupboards, the wardrobes, paperwork, garage, loft space, anywhere where you have materialistic things. Sell, give away or throw away anything you no longer use, love or enjoy. You are clearing space in your head as you do this, you have less to worry about.

Is your house too big for you? Do you worry about all of the maintenance? Are the running expenses becoming too high for your income? Downsize, only have what you are going to use. Why have a four bedroom house if there are only either one or two of you living there? Extra heating, rates, water rates. Really look at your lifestyle.

You will be amazed at how much stress downsizing gets rid of and you will have spare cash and time to go on holidays or to do things that you would like to do.

This also goes for your car, how many garages you have, sheds, loft space. It can save you a fortune.

Four years ago, I moved from a large four bedroomed house with a double garage to a rented two up, two down. No garage, no loft and no shed, with just a paved area to put my bistro table and two chairs on, outside. No maintenance, anything needs doing, I ring my landlord and I have to say what a very good one he is too! I don't have to worry if there's adverse weather conditions, no fences to worry about or ridge tiles, I lie in bed and I can sleep knowing all is well.

Do I miss anything.....NO! I am the happiest I have ever been in all of my life. I am content. I have time to enjoy coffeeing with friends, my hobbies or walking Alfie, my little dog, in the surrounding countryside. I tell people, I have won the lottery of life. Try it! I'm sure you will to.

Start de-cluttering today!

Rent Or Buy?

So do you rent or buy?

I have always owned my own home until a few years ago. I had sold my house to a first time buyer, who wanted to move in, in six weeks. So I decided I more or less knew where I wanted to move to, I thought I would look for somewhere to rent then when something came up to buy, I would buy it.

I had made an appointment to view a house and the night before the viewing, I showed Steven, my elder son, the advert on line and he pointed out another property, which I liked the look of. I rang and made an appointment 9 a.m. the next morning. I had just put the telephone down, when the phone started ringing. It was the estate agent of the other property, cancelling my viewing.

I picked my friend Jean up and we set off on our journey, twenty six miles into the country. I had arranged to meet the landlord, outside of Barclays Bank and as we were waiting there, Jean and I wondered as to just where the property could possibly be.

My landlord arrived and pointed out the property on the opposite side of the road. I was not impressed. It had to be one of the most ugliest buildings in the town which has some beautiful stone built houses.

Lesson …. Do not judge a book by it's cover, as when we got inside it was quirky, spacious, it had old beams and the most important fact was it had a great feel to it. I knew instantly the moment I set foot in it, that I could be happy there and the icing on the cake was when I looked out of the bedroom window I could see animals in the not so distant field, between the gap of the houses opposite. I was two minutes away from all of the amenities, in fact everything on my wish list had been ticked.

God had answered my prayers, maybe not as I thought He would, but everything was perfect. I also had no worries about big maintenance bills. It was brilliant. I had a sense of freedom, as if there was anything I didn't like I could move at the drop of a hat.

I have never been more content or happy in my life. For me it's rent every time from now on. I have no worries, no stress, if anything goes wrong my landlord is just a phone call away.

I have money in the bank giving me security and I can enjoy what I have worked all my life for.

Yoga

Have you ever participated in Yoga? I was persuaded a while ago, by a very dear friend, to try it. Yes I struggled at times and yes I'd manage so much better if my arms and legs were six inches longer but I have to say, try it.

My yoga class commenced at 10 a.m. and I have to confess that by 10:30 a.m. I would be looking at the clock on the wall opposite, thinking I'll never make it to 11 a.m. but then suddenly Anne, our teacher, would announce it was time for relaxation. My friend and I would exchange glances and think thank goodness, we've made it through another class without showing ourselves up.

It was time to put our socks and jumpers on then lie down and prepare ourselves for the relaxation, going wherever it would take us. Sometimes we didn't want to come back, it was so enjoyable, just lying there in our own little world but coffee was calling at our local cafe, No.10, which was very conveniently situated just off the Market Square, where the yoga class was held.

It was then time to exercise our tongues, with a good old catch up. First on the agenda would be how the lady with the extra long arms and legs got herself into such positions and how we'd do so much better if we were that much taller but there again we wouldn't have so much fun.

I must say my friends and I, would at times, hardly dare to look at each other, whilst doing the class, in case we burst out laughing.

One such time was when we had to put one leg up on to a table/radiator/chair, whichever you could manage and then bend towards the floor. One of my friends looked at me with that look 'She's got to be joking!' Then looked away as she knew we'd get the fit of giggles and the position we were in, would also see the two of us having an accident, seen as we are ladies of a certain age, who's bladder is maybe not as strong as one would hope it to be.

Advice :- Start doing yoga in your 20's when you are supple and it will keep you supple in your later years, of course that is only if you keep it up.

Seville

Talking about getting the giggles, I must tell you about the time my friend and I went to Seville on a Walking, Writing and Meditation retreat.

We arrived at the Bon Vino, where we were spending our next seven days and nights, in the hills of Andalusia. We had met Elaine who was taking the retreat and two other ladies, who like us, were also on the retreat.

We'd enjoyed a delicious meal, cooked by Jeanie, our hostess, who along with Sam, our host, owned the estate which was set in 750 acres of woodland. Idyllic!

We'd had a great day, Sam had met us in Seville, he had taken us on a pub crawl to show us the parts of Seville, tourists just don't get to see. First stop was a convent where he purchased biscuits for our tea. He knocked at this tiny door in the wall and a nun answered it. He asked her if he could buy a bag of biscuits. She went away and returned with not one but two bags of biscuits. She gave the second bag free because he had been kind enough to purchase the first bag of biscuits.

We stopped off at the fresh fish stall in the local market, tasting the fresh prawns amongst other seafood which to be honest I couldn't bare the site of, never mind put in my mouth. I am not very adventurous when it comes to food. Sam ordered wine from the wine merchants which hopefully would last the week and then we were on our way.

On our pub tour around Seville we were given samples of parma ham & smoked tuna amongst other local delicacies and the local sherry which was a must.

By 4 p.m. we were in the people carrier on our way to our destination, feeling somewhat apprehensive but very excited, as we just did not know what the week had in store for us.

Their estate with the 750 acres of woodland astounded us and their home which was very mediterranean, looked so much older than what it really was.

Thirty two years ago Jeanie and Sam had arrived in Spain, they'd bought the land and after much thought and consideration, decided where they were going to build their home. Jeanie, who had just given birth to their son, had used the pram, with chalk on it's wheels, to draw out on the earth the plans for the house. They had built a most beautiful house which looked 300 years old, not just 32 and it was so quirky, just like them.

Anyhow, I've set the scene, my friend and I were staying in a room on the second floor and after supper and after an exciting but exhausting day, we decided it was time to retire to our room. We struggled up the five flights of stairs but when we did arrive, somewhat out of breath, we found great difficulty allocating the light switch in our room. I told you it was quirky.

The light switch was not where you would normally find a light switch. I had remembered seeing two plugs in between our beds earlier in the day, when we had unpacked. So I fumbled around in the dark, found one and plugged it in. Just then the main light came on, so I thought no more about it. We got washed and ready for bed, said goodnight and switched off the light.

Well you know what it's like, your first night on holiday, I tossed and turned and must have eventually dropped off into a deep sleep when suddenly the light went on, my friend was screaming that she was on fire. She was screaming to me "Feel, feel under my pillow, it's roasting!"

I got out of bed and felt it. It indeed was red hot. Unknowingly, I had plugged in the electric blanket, when I thought I'd switched on the light. The temperature in the room must have been in the 20's, she certainly did not need an electric blanket on.

Well we laughed and laughed, eventually we switched the light off but I kept thinking about what had just happened and bursting into a fit of giggles. Even today, if it comes up in conversation we start laughing.

The next morning we had to write in our journal for ten minutes with whatever came into our heads. Well I was sitting there, the tears streaming down my face and I was having difficulty writing. My friend, in a cross voice said, "I know what you are writing about!"

Well we had to tell the others what had happened the night before and before long we were all laughing, including my friend.

We had many laughs that holiday and it was one of our most memorable holidays. I had spotted a small advert about the retreat advertised in Woman and Home magazine and had thought, 'Why not!' So as the saying goes, feel the fear and do it anyway. Sometimes when we don't know what's coming, turns out to be so special.

Just be careful which plug you plug in!

Snow

I don't know about you, but as soon as it starts snowing, I feel revitalised. I woke up one morning at 7:45 a.m. to find it was raining, so I went back to bed.

I woke again at 9:45 a.m. looked out of the window to see a blanket of snow. I quickly got ready and took my dog Alfie, for an extra long walk.

Afterwards I went and did my shopping and got lots of jobs done, which had been waiting days to be done. I had so much energy.

Is it psychological, does my brain think yes it's winter but spring is around the corner..........who knows!

I certainly do have more energy when it snows.

Sixty One

I just happened to say to a friend that I would be 61 this year, in fact, in one month. My friend told me that I didn't look it! To which I replied that I also didn't act it!

Whenever I can, I try to connect with my inner child, I have fun, go on adventures and on the whole, enjoy life, each and every day. Don't get me wrong, I do have down days, but more often than not, they are my character building days or at least that's what I like to call them.

There is normally a reason for them and I work through what is the reason why I'm feeling like I am. I then give thanks for whatever it was, that had been brought to my attention. I was able to do something about it and put whatever was troubling me, to rest with thanks.

Photographs

Are you like me? Have you drawers and drawers of photos just waiting to be sorted. You have blurred ones, two of the same, photos of people you can't even remember, views where you have forgotten where you were when you took them, animals!

Do you get where I'm coming from?

Well I am pleased to say I have made a start, my goal being to make memory books for my two sons, especially for my elder son, as he has no memory of his childhood since we divorced, when he was fifteen. I would like both of them to realise that it wasn't all bad, we did have good fun as a family.

I have to say, when you decide to start sorting, make sure you have nothing urgent needs doing, because the hours will just go, as you relive the memories, smile, maybe have a few tears but one thing you will have, is enjoyed however long you spent sorting them.

Friendships

Have you got that friend that is really hard work? You do all the running! Well have you thought, just maybe, your friendship has run it's course, it's time to move on.

Relationships are just like wardrobes / drawers / cupboards, every now and again it's good to have a spring clean. Let go of the relationships which aren't working, to enable you to either spend more time on the relationships that are or maybe you just need to make some space so that new relationships can come into your life.

We are all growing and sometimes we outgrow who we are with and need to let go, to enable us to grow and move forward with our lives. If we don't then we get stuck and aren't able to move at all.

We just don't know what is waiting to enter our lives.

Worry!

Fear, worry, anxiety.......the more you think about it, the worse it gets. I learnt a long time ago to give it all up.

I always give it up to God but if God is not for you then you can give it up to the Universe. What we have to realise is that there is a bigger picture, which we can't see and it will all work out for the highest good in the end, it doesn't matter how big or small your problem is, please give it up.

It does work, the power of prayer and having faith. Just remember it might not be as you would want it to turn out but it will work out better than you could have ever imagined, if you let go.

F.E.A.R. ....FALSE EVIDENCE APPEARING REAL! Believe, trust then let go!

Be Careful What You Wish For!

When I was sitting, at the beginning of 2016, I thought about how I wanted to start writing, sort out all of my paperwork, cupboards, wardrobes, photos, diaries to be gone through, computer sorted, books to read, the list goes on. I asked the Universe for space in my life to be able to achieve all of this.

On the 18th January I became ill and after two weeks, I discovered I had viral pneumonia. I was put on a high dose of steroids for three weeks. This meant that although I was extremely breathless, I was very alert, needing only a few hours sleep, some nights I got as little as forty minutes sleep.

I was ill for two months in total, which gave me all the time I needed to do a lot of the above and get everything in my house organised. It also gave me a lot of time to ponder on what I wanted in life and who are my trusted friends. It has been an eye opener to say the least and it has made me think about what my priorities are in life.

Note:- In holistic terms pneumonia means loosing the will to live.

Had I? My mum had died two years previously and I used to spend a lot of time with her. Both my sons had moved to Dubai and after my visit in December 2015, I realised they were both settled in their lives, they both had new families, this being their circle of friends. Did I feel redundant?

Maybe! What did I have to live for? It certainly made me stop and think when I read this definition and I decided yes I did want to live, as I still had things I wanted to achieve in life plus I want to hopefully see my grandchildren grow up, if and when I have any. I also want to be there for my sons, as my mum had been there for me, unfortunately my dad died when I was twenty seven.

This also happened to me three years previously, when I sold my house and was considering moving to the countryside. My elder son asked where was he going to go if I moved and I told him that he was very welcome to come with me but this time, I was moving to where I wanted to live and not to where he thought I should move to.

Two weeks later a 'Mystery Shopper' walked in to where he worked and offered him a job in Dubai, working for Harley Davidson. He took it and has a very happy life in Dubai. Five months later my younger son, was offered a job also in Dubai and moved out there at the end of August 2014. They live just a few hundred metres away from each other.

I also realised that what I had set out to do, I had accomplished. I had raised two very independent boys. So yes if we leave it to the Universe, things work out so much better.

Illness

You normally find, like everything in life, that good comes out of being ill. We are given time to heal and during that time we are able to sit quietly and think, we can sort out paperwork which has built up in our busy lives. We can take time out to read, do crafts etc. even just sit, relax and watch a favourite T.V. programme.

You also realise just what a fantastic support system you have in place. There's no need to worry, life goes on, you just have to step off the treadmill for a while, it'll still go round without you.

I was amazed at how my dog was walked three times a day, my shopping got done, I had visitors to help pass the time away. I had someone to take me to hospital for scans and appointments. I did not have to worry, all I had to do was rest and let my body heal itself.

We sometimes wonder why we get ill but we should look at the bigger picture. Maybe it's a way of slowing us down and giving us time to reflect on where we are going and what we are doing with our lives.

You hear people say when they've experienced ill health/tragedy, that it was a life changing experience. They have had time to take stock, get rid of what wasn't working and start to do more of what they enjoy doing.

67

They appreciate life more. This in the end makes them feel happier and healthier.

As my health started to improve I realised how productive I'd been whilst I had been ill. I had read some very good books. I'd knitted a cardigan, a jumper, scarf, a dozen dishcloths for my local W.I. sales table. I had completed my challenge I had given myself of knitting myself a pair of socks. In fact I had enjoyed doing it so much, I had knitted a second pair. I'd baked and made tasty biscuits and cake for my friends to have with their coffee when they popped in. I'd watched some interesting programmes on T.V. and got hints on how to tweak my wardrobe, what best savings were around and I also realised just how happy I was in my home. Yes, I made a few mental plans for when I was fully recovered of what I wanted to do in the house.

So all in all, the first few months of 2016 were certainly not wasted, anything but. I got my paperwork sorted and what needed to go out, shredded, a new address book written up and my recipe book from 1982 re-wrote and all the pieces of paper with recipes on, copied and got rid of. Also recipes I no longer used, omitted. I past recipes on to my friends and I also found new recipes which I was eager to try.

I baked one day, my incentive was a cake stall at my local W.I.'s Soup and Stottie day. I couldn't attend but what I could do, was contribute. It took my mind off how I was feeling and I felt good when I had a table full of goodies.

I even asked my neighbour, who had had Alfie out for a walk, to come back and have lunch with me, because whilst I was waiting for my cakes to cook, I had made a pan of broth and baked a bacon joint.

I had the pleasure of her company and in return I was able to give a busy single mum, a little bit of time out. We sat and chattered and she appreciated having her meal cooked for her and I had also enjoyed her company.

I sorted wardrobes and drawers out, only keeping what I felt good in and gave the rest to charity along with all the things I no longer used, including books I had read and things I had bought but had never used.

I went through photos, sending ones off to people who might like old photos of themselves, destroying photos of people I had met on holiday years ago and couldn't remember their names, got rid of blurred ones, scenic ones, even getting rid of some of my family ones where I had similar shots, just keeping the best ones.

When I came to the end of my clear out, I felt I could go through it all again and get rid of more. I have found the less I have, the less I have to worry about, clean, or find space for. It has cleared my life, giving me more time to spend on the things I want to do and enjoy doing, which at the end of the day makes me happy and content. The less I have the happier I am.

Note; When you read a book or magazine pass it on to someone else, for them to read and enjoy. Upon purchasing new clothes or shoes get rid of an old item or pair which you no longer wear. Stop clogging your life up. Even go through your emails, texts and delete what are no longer required. It all clogs up your life.

Good luck and enjoy clearing out your life, it's amazing what you find, the memories that come back, I bet you will find it really enjoyable. Start with one box, a drawer or a wardrobe, don't look at the bigger picture or else you will feel quite daunted by it all.

Dreams

Never give up on your dreams and wishes, whatever they are and no matter how small because one day they could come true.

2014 - November. I visited a Lulu Guinness shop for the first time whilst visiting an arcade in London. As a lover of red lipstick and the colour black, I fell in love with her designer bags and hoped one day to own one!

In the December I went to see my boys in Dubai and hinted that if ever they were stuck with what to buy me, I would love the black patent handbag on the top shelf in the Lulu Guinness shop in the Souk Madinat Jumeirah.

A year went by, I visited my sons again and twice I visited the Lulu Guinness shop but came away empty handed, thinking it was too expensive.

Whilst I was ill I was sitting one night, when it came into my head to go on to the Lulu Guinness website.

The bag I so desired had 50% off and I was guided to look for a promotional code where I got a further 10% off.

I was a very happy bunny, my dream had indeed come true and just what I would have liked for my birthday, which was only two weeks away.

Healing And Wholeness

I am not at peace, so I must have made the wrong decision.

It was me who made that decision but I can change my mind.

If I change my mind, I will be at peace.

If we pray to God/Universe we will receive help in making the right decision.

I decide to let God/Universe make my decision for me.

When we are at peace, then we know we have chosen the correct path. If we are struggling, then we know we are using free will which will almost certainly create a character building period.

We must stop and ask God/Universe for guidance, if we are quiet and still, we will be shown what we must do to get back on the straight and narrow. Always, always go with your gut feeling, as this is your guidance.

I have learnt that it does no good offloading your problems onto your family and friends, as they will give you their view and possibly lead you in a different direction to the one you should be on.

We hand over our power to other people instead of giving it up to God /the Universe for it to be solved in the best possible way, for the highest good of all concerned.

Instead, if you have a problem, whatever it may be, it might just be a niggling worry, STOP! PRAY! WAIT!

You will see that whatever has been troubling you, will be sorted in a much better way than you could possibly have dreamed of.

This is one of the biggest lessons I have learnt in my life and I have to admit, it has taken me until I was sixty one to actually put it into practice. It has taken time but as the saying goes, better late than never.

I hope you try to. Believe me it definitely works.

Birthdays

All my life, I have arranged things, the food, where to go for my birthdays, who is helping me celebrate it. I always felt that I would be disappointed, if others planned it for me. I did not think that they were aware of my preferences.

Then when I was ill in 2016 and because I couldn't be bothered with anything, I didn't expect anything and I ended up having one of the best ever birthdays.

Friends came and went. I had phone calls, my eldest son, Face timed me and talked to me for an hour. My younger son, Face timed me in the evening, when his girlfriend came to visit me and we had a wonderful three way conversation. I received flowers in the post, my very good friends and neighbours made me birthday cakes. Janet had made me a cake with a Lulu Guinness bag on it - fantastic!

The day was low key, very touching and at the end of it, I felt truly loved.

Lesson learnt:- Don't try to control your life, it turns out so much better when left to chance.

Working

I never realised until I was doing some reading on The Journey that I felt so angry that out of all the women in my family, I was the only one who had worked for so long. My mum, sister and sister-in-law had stopped working when they got married. I worked for thirty four years, then studied on and off for the next ten years whilst being around for my ageing mum and helping people.

I couldn't understand how I was always coming down with some sort of illness. I would just start something then I would become ill. I thought it mustn't be the right direction I had to go in. But all along it was my subconscious saying I didn't want to work!

After having my epiphany I gave thanks for those thirty four years working because it has given me a much more interesting life. I have had some fabulous holidays, met some very interesting people and I am now on my spiritual journey, helping people wherever I can.

2006-2008 I had become very friendly with a lady from the church I regularly attended. We became quite close as her illness was getting worse, she was suffering from secondary cancer. Due to my sister being quite poorly quite a lot during her life, I have a lot of empathy for people who are ill.

This friend happened to tell me one day when I had taken her to get measured for her prosthesis, that wherever we went, she had noticed that I was able to help people. This had gone unnoticed to me until she brought it to my attention, I just do it automatically.

It made me realise that maybe that was why I had gone through so much trauma and tragedy in my life, it enables me to have empathy with others. It makes so much difference when you understand another's pain.

Holy Week

I noticed Spirit working with me. The more time I spend working on my spiritual journey, the more Spirit works with me. It is happening so much, I am learning not to discuss problems with friends and family, instead I go and sit quietly in my bedroom and talk to God and the Angels.

This is a summary of what has occurred this week:-

I prayed and asked for help with my eating, as I had gained a half a stone in weight, which I could ill afford. Afterwards I noticed I was going to the cupboards if I was feeling peckish and it was the healthy options which caught my eye, not the biscuits or crisps.

I was exercising more, walking that little bit further, doing those extra jobs in the house. Everything to help burn up those unwanted calories.

We can ask the angels to help us with anything in our daily lives.

My friend rang to say the priest who joins us on our annual pilgrimage, was going to be preaching for the week, at my old parish church and she invited me to stay over on Easter Saturday so that I could go and listen and enjoy his amazing sermons.

All positive!

I Do Matter

I did go and stay with my friend. We went together to the services and listened to the priest giving his sermon.

I have heard him speak on quite a few occasions, I find his sermons enthralling and he always has a fantastic way of putting his message across to his congregation. I had actually travelled twenty six miles to hear him and it had been worth every mile.

I sat listening to his sermon, waiting for his message to connect with me and then he said it, "You do matter!"

The more I thought about it, the more I realised that God wouldn't have put me on this Earth if there wasn't a reason for my life.

Yes every one of us matters and I think we need to give ourselves credit that we do have a mission here on Earth, even if we don't realise it and at the same time realise that we are loved, God loves us, as does the Universe. We are not meant to suffer. We should be living Heaven on Earth.

Bank Holidays

Easter Sunday, after church I had a coffee with my friends then headed for home.

My head was telling me I should be going out for my lunch as it was Easter but instead I was going home to celebrate Easter Sunday on my own.

It then struck me that of all those people who were with families maybe some of them didn't want to be there. They would be thinking of all the things they would have preferred doing, instead of keeping family traditions and all eating together.

It made me grateful, I have choices and I decided to change my thoughts.

For lunch I had a toasted hot cross bun with cheese which was most enjoyable, then I sat and caught up with my T.V. programmes I had previously recorded.

I relaxed and enjoyed doing some knitting, before I took Alfie for a brisk walk. It was bitterly cold and because I felt energised when I came back, I sorted out one of my wardrobes. I felt I had done a good job as I tied the handles of a full bag of clothing ready to go to the charity shop.

The lesson I learnt today was change your thought patterns. You can do anything, at any time, on any day. Nothing is set in stone.

Loosing A Loved One

Are we ever prepared or ready to loose a loved one? Are we ever ready to cut the chord that attaches us to them?

I had a visit from an old school friend, whose wife had died not long ago. I could see that his grief was still very raw and painful when he talked about her but one thing he said was "She was ready to go but no way was I ready to let her go."

I think we all find it really hard to detach ourselves from people and material things but if we can, it frees our loved ones and ourselves and opens us up to what life has to offer. It is hard to become detached but if we can, it eases us from worry and stress, amongst other things too.

We have to realise that each and every one of us has our own path and journey and sometimes we have to go it alone.

I found this out when my ninety three year old mum, who I had been caring for, passed over.

It was a huge lesson and I realised it was 'My Time' to start and love myself and do what I wanted to do, as I had always put myself last. It was very hard and uncomfortable at first but the longer I am on my own the more I enjoy my life.

Life

Life is not a long vacation, it is a lesson on how to love and without love we are nothing. We get lots of opportunities to learn in our lifetime. We continue until the day we die.

We know when we are on our Divine pathway, as things go according to plan. Whereas, if we choose Free Will and decide we want to do things differently, then we could come across many trials and learn many lessons on our way. The choice is ours.

We don't loose out if we choose Free Will, we just learn more and with every lesson, we learn to become stronger, more patient, more co-operative etc. It makes us the person we become, normally a much better one at that.

Our Children And Letting Go

One day I popped to see my neighbour, when she opened the door she said "You must have known, they've (the angels) sent you!"

When I asked what was wrong, she became very tearful, her daughter, aged twelve at the time, was wanting to go to town to meet her friends.

My neighbour was mortified about having to let go of control and the thought of her little girl getting older and not needing her so much was unbearable.

We must, as mothers, realise that our bodies are a vessel which our children use, to be born into this world and we have to learn that our children aren't ever our possession. They are truly a gift from God.

Our job is to love and protect them and teach them how to be independent, so much so, that as they get older and more responsible they will be wanting to leave home and live their own lives.

They will love you all the more for doing so. Smothering them could possibly drive them away.

Slowing Down And Enjoying The Little Things In Life.

One thing I noticed when I was recovering from the bout of pneumonia, was that all of the time I had been on my own enjoying peace, tranquility and literally the small things in life, which included daily meditation, not once had I felt lonely.

And so as I returned to normality, whatever normality is, I started to think before I agreed to commit to anything or to go anywhere, as I was enjoying my peaceful life. A life where I could dip in or out of everyday life, whenever I chose to.

I realised I enjoy just sitting in silence, amazed at what my mind brings to my attention. I find pleasure sitting with Alfie on my knee, just sitting relaxing, stroking and cuddling him or reading a good book. I'm sure he enjoys it to.

Such simple things that are so enjoyable and yet they cost nothing and I get so much pleasure from doing them.

Even just giving yourself time to go for a walk, to notice the birds singing. I see a lot of people walking with their headphones in, I think it is so sad, they just aren't aware of what they are missing! Look up at the trees can you see which birds are singing, you might even spot a squirrel lurking somewhere up in the branches. Take time to notice the trees, what type they are, take note of their bark, the branches, are they out in blossom, are there buds on the branches.

Then look up at the sky, can you see any clouds? Is it a clear blue sky? Are there different shades of blue? If there are clouds, what type of clouds? Are they featherlike, fluffy, storm clouds or pinky grey snow clouds? What colours can you see in the clouds? Imagine painting them, what colours would you use? Can you see a face or a creature in one of them? They are fascinating! Also if it has been raining can you see a rainbow?

Fill yourself with the wonders of nature and notice how your heart sings. Mine does when I see the spring flowers, especially when I find the first snowdrop, I know Spring is just around the corner. You might be lucky to see a new born lamb in the field with it's mother or there may be a couple of lambs frolicking in the distance, just enjoying being alive. Notice the birds foraging for twigs, feathers, moss, anything to make their nests cosy.

When I have been out for a walk, I come home feeling so happy and grateful for my day, I am glad to be alive and so grateful I have been given this time to appreciate nature at it's best. I feel as if I have won the lottery of life. I hope you will to.

Money

I decided a few years ago to write down every penny that I spent and on what I had spent it on. As I had been very lax of late, maybe because I had so much more important things occupying my mind. What brought it all to my attention was when I received my annual credit card summary, it made me aware of just how much I had been spending and what I had been spending it on, without realising. It is so easy using a card, whereas if you pay in cash you take more notice.

I started to realise over the coming months just where and what I needed to cut back on, the first things were coffees and lunches out.

The second thing was 'The New Season' watching T.V., also being persuaded by the media that we needed new colours and new styles etc., adding to our wardrobes.

Why, oh why, can't we just be individuals revamping what we have in our wardrobes, creating our own styles instead of someone else telling us what we have to wear and for what occasion.

By wearing different tops with skirts and trousers, mixing and matching, making different looks, with a piece of jewellery or a scarf! I have decided not to fall for that one again. Okay buy one or two bits what might catch your eye and what you really like but not a whole wardrobe!

And the third thing is food! Why not shop on an afternoon or a Monday when the shops have items reduced. Have fun cutting back.

The Mind

It is strange how we always think that our addictions, habits etc., are part of who we are and that we cannot change them.

BUT WE CAN!

With regards to food I find that I now choose healthy options. I have no desire to eat 'rubbish.' When we have such thoughts, you know what I mean, that 'little voice' in your head saying "Go on have another chocolate biscuit" even though you have just finished your evening meal and aren't really hungry. It is because you are bored. Go and find something to do to take your mind off food.

I have also become more aware of what I am spending money on which is making me think twice before I make a purchase. When you hear that little voice in your head saying "Go on buy another pair of shoes, they are in the sale and they are cheap!"

It doesn't matter that you have at least twenty pairs of shoes in your wardrobe, some of which never get worn. Why? Because they are too tight, too uncomfortable, you no longer like the colour, whatever the reason, just stop your thoughts and change them to

'You know what, I don't need them.' I love myself and I am going to use that money wisely, maybe on a pamper session, or a trip to the hairdressers.

Spend your money on something you can appreciate. Instead of eating and regretting it or putting the item in a cupboard and forgetting it is even there.

If you have a headache or a pain try sending love to that part of your body instead of immediately going to the cupboard for some painkillers. You could also try drinking a glass of water, it is quite possible you are dehydrated.

We can do lots of things to change our lives. Maybe the first thing is to start putting yourself first, have that conversation with yourself and do what you know, is best for you.

You are worth it and you are beautiful as you are, God created you perfect and it's only someone else's opinion that you are not. Each day look into the mirror and say to yourself, "I love you." Slowly but surely you will start and believe it.

An old lady once said to me "It is time to put yourself first, you are No.1. No more putting everyone else first."

She was right, I had always put everyone before myself. I had given but very rarely received. We think it's being selfish if we put ourselves first but in actual fact it isn't. If we do put ourselves first, then other people will learn from us to put themselves first, just like the ripple on a pond.

It's all about balance. When we give, we must learn to receive too. Good luck!

Springtime

I feel so grateful and fortunate that I both have the time and the inclination to go walking plus I have Alfie as my personal trainer.

I live in a town that is surrounded by countryside, five minutes walk and I'm walking along by the beck with the ducks bobbing about or five minutes the other way finds me walking along the riverside and woodland. I am living an ideal life.

Today as I walked, I noticed a stillness, it was still cold but the icy wind had dropped. I think nature was making the most of it, birds busily furrowing for twigs etc., to build their nests. I saw one bird, I wasn't sure what it was, as I was too far away to recognise it but what I did see, was it taking a twig and disappearing down someone's chimney pot. I hoped the people whose chimney pot it was, didn't light their fire until the bird's fledglings had flown the nest.

A robin came out of the bushes to greet me and in the middle of the river, waiting on a stone, was a dipper, waiting to literally dive in and get some food. The lambs were snuggled into their mothers in the field keeping themselves warm. There were some in the distance frolicking and playing.

In the next field the 'ladies in waiting' were waiting patiently to lamb. I noticed that they were baaing away and all heading in one direction. When I stopped to look at where they were heading, I noticed the farmer bringing their breakfast, a bale of hay.

The river was quite low considering the many downpours we had had the previous day. The springtime flowers, gently swaying in the breeze. I so love them, the bright yellow daffodils giving us an insight into the bright sunny days of summer to come. All the spring flowers are vibrant in colour to cheer us up after the long, dark, cold winter.

Gosh, I am so grateful to be alive and so lucky to have the time and inclination to take Alfie on these woodland walks along the riverside and to be able to experience Spring at it's best. Noticing the buds starting to appear on the branches tells me that it won't be long before they will be opening out into beautiful green leaves. It is so good to be at one with nature and to just live in the moment.

Change Your Thoughts

One day, for some unknown reason, I felt quite low, whilst I was eating my breakfast and so I stopped what I was doing, I said a prayer of thanks for my food and I asked the Angels to be with me, guide and protect me and prepare my journey throughout the day with blessings.

I took Alfie for his walk and gave thanks for everything I saw and as I walked words for a poem came into my head. I was very grateful, as I needed a poem for our next W.I. meeting. When I got back home, I sat quietly with a cup of coffee and the words came flowing back. Within ten minutes my poem was written.

I made my lunch then went off to the local Knit and Natter group. My friends weren't able to go, as they had gone off to a meeting but I need not have worried as there was a lovely group of ladies there. We chattered, knitting as we were chattering and after an hour we stopped for coffee and cake, all for the cost of one pound for two hours pleasure.

At 3:00 p.m. I made my way home, by which time my heart was a lot lighter and I was truly grateful.

I had literally just sat down, at home, when there was a knock at my door and an old friend from where I used to live, was standing there. She had been on a guided walk and they had ended up at our local pub. She very kindly had come to see if I would like to join them for a drink, which I did. I wasn't there long but it was lovely to have a catch up and I enjoyed my tonic water. My heart was singing by the time I walked home.

I just had time to take Alfie for his evening walk, I finished what I was knitting, painted my nails, had a shower and I was ready to go again. This time I was off to the monthly meeting of the Supper Club. We had excellent food, I was sat with lovely warm hearted people and I had a most enjoyable evening.

I went home and gave thanks for a fantastic day. What had started on a low had definitely ended on a high.

If ever you feel in a low mood when you get up on a morning, just stop, give thanks for everything that you are grateful for and take the time to change your thoughts and send a prayer up asking for an enjoyable day.

I always give thanks and count my blessings at the beginning and end of each day. This enables me to start and end each day on a positive note.

Public Transport

A couple of years ago I was told by a consultant that I wasn't able to drive for six weeks and so when I got back home I began to think up a plan.

I thought about it and thought I would be adventurous and give the public transport a go. I was meeting up with some of my W.I. crowd that evening to play darts at our local pub, so I asked the fortunate ladies, who owned bus passes, what time and where could I get the local bus into our local city.

They were all very eager to tell me, unfortunately all at the same time. I thought I had got the gist of it all and so I planned my adventure for the very next day.

I was up early, showered, dressed and yes I thought seen as I was going into the city, I would even put my make-up on.

Alfie walked, I set off for the bus, I was nice and early but had I made a mistake? I had decided to go 'colour co-ordinated' in other words my navy mack, instead of my sensible warm, stormproof, winter coat with a hood!

The wind was icy cold but after ten minutes wait, the bus arrived. I sat beside a lovely lady who informed me that just three miles up the Dale, they had a covering of snow. I was not surprised, the chill factor must have been well below zero.

This kind lady told me the number of my next bus and where to get it. Great I felt quite elated, things were going well. After another fifteen minutes wait, the bus eventually arrived, I was off on the final leg of my journey.

A nice gentleman got on the bus and sat beside me. He was, I would say in his early seventies and had just moved from Alston, to be near civilisation. Well that's what he said! It was also his first time on the bus, so we were both 'bus virgins' so to speak.

I arrived into Durham, one hour and fifteen minutes after I had left home, this journey would have normally taken me just under thirty minutes in my car. BUT! I was on an adventure, I wasn't in a hurry, I certainly was not stressed and my journey had been very sociable.

So, so far, so good. I made my way to British Home Stores, I had a top which I wanted to return. On my way to the till, I saw another top I would like instead of it and so I made my way to the counter with both tops.

When I got there, the assistant said she would have to phone to see if she could exchange my top. This was due to the fact that BHS had announced the previous evening that they had gone into administration. To be truthful, that was the reason why I had made my mind up to make the journey. I had heard the announcement on the 6 o'clock news the previous evening.

After a long conversation on the telephone, it was agreed that I could indeed change my top for something else but the top I was exchanging it for was cheaper and they could only exchange for the same price.

So off I went in search of something for the price difference. I decided on some knickers, you can never have enough knickers or at least they wouldn't come in wrong.

Back at the counter, I was told there was a difference of fifteen pence. I ended up having to buy a Cadbury Creme Egg, which I detest but I was meeting my son's girlfriend, Grace, for lunch and so I would give it to her, as she liked them. What a palaver!

Well at least I was able to exchange my top and I ended up with a top, two pairs of knickers and a Cadbury Cream Egg for the same price.

I got outside and the black clouds, which I had been watching from inside of the bus, had decided to empty their load over Durham. It was snowing! Rather heavily at that, no hood, no umbrella and not a shop in sight which sold umbrellas. I was soaked by the time I got to Grace's workplace.

My day was getting better by the minute or maybe not. We chattered for a while, then went out for lunch. Whilst I was enjoying my hot corned beef pie, coleslaw, chutney and salad, I asked how her recent visit to Dubai, visiting Paul, had gone.

She told me, she had been for two job interviews whilst she was there and had been offered both jobs. She had chosen which one she thought would be the best and she was moving out in the July.

I was gutted! Not only would I not have her popping in for a chat or seeing her when I went to Durham but my son had less reasons to come back to England.

Lunch finished, we said farewell and we went our separate ways. By this time I had managed to purchase an umbrella but yes, you have guessed it, five minutes after purchasing one, the sun came out. I found my way back to the bus station and the stand where my bus was leaving from, only to find out that I had just missed my bus.

Twenty five minutes to wait! I found a cafe, had a coffee and thought I had better visit the ladies room, as I had at least an hour before I would get home.

Well, thank goodness, the bus arrived on time, again I had a chatty guy sit beside me, to enrich my journey. The bus seemed to get to Crook, where I had to change, in no time, 2:35 p.m. The next bus to Wolsingham, wasn't until 3:15 p.m.

The wind had got up and the temperature had dropped considerably as the sun was now going down, it felt a lot colder. I wandered around the local shops until eventually my bus came.

I got home at 3:40 p.m. nearly six hours after I had left that morning. I couldn't believe it. I had learnt a lot from this adventure.

Firstly, buy a day return. It had cost me over twelve pounds and I later found out that I could have had my journey for half of the price.

Secondly, plan my full journey, bus times and times of connecting buses.

Thirdly be very grateful for my car, the ability to be able to drive it and the time it saves me.

Yes the bus is less stressful, you don't have to find a parking space and it was very sociable and if I add up wear and tear on the car, petrol and parking fees they would, I would imagine most likely work out about the same.

So if you have all the time in the world, fancy an adventure and people to talk to then by all means go on public transport.

Mental Health

The programme 'Loose Women' had just launched a 'Talk About It' campaign, saying 1 in 4 of us have some sort of mental health issue each year.

Whilst watching the programme, it touched a sore spot and I started to cry. I not only was crying, I was sobbing and I asked myself "Why?"

My answers were, I felt lonely, I miss my boys and my mum. I have no partner and therefore no-one to truly confide in.

Ester Ranzen says the 70-80 year olds are lonely! I say "What about the single parents, divorced, widowed before their time, single career minded people who have devoted their lives to work and when it's there no more, are lost, and people who have had to move away and as yet have not made friends."

There are so many younger people sitting in houses all over the world, feeling very isolated and lonely. Yes we have friends and neighbours but what happens on weekends and Bank Holidays when our friends are with their husbands and families? It is so hard!

Then there's Mother's Day, birthdays and every other day come to that, when you are made to feel like Billy No Mates.

I am a generous person who loves to give and I am also a mother who is now redundant, I have no-one to look after or give to, it breaks my heart. The nation calls it 'Empty Nest Syndrome!' We give our lives to our children and then we have to make them independent enough so they leave the nest.

We now have to live our lives, re-create ourselves, find out who this daughter/son, wife/husband, mother/father actually is. What has been lying dormant inside of us, just waiting for the right time to evolve.

It's like a chrysalis waiting for the beautiful butterfly to emerge.

Pensions/ Money

The Government has changed the Pension rule, so although we have paid into the pot, they have decided we can't have it, well not until I personally am almost sixty seven.

I used my savings and equity released from a lifetime mortgage to bring up my sons and care for my mum. My savings disappeared fast and just before my house was sold, it had been on the market for three years, I prayed to God that He would find me a solution to my money problems.

My mum went into a home, the next day I sold my house and whilst I was waiting for the funds to come through, I borrowed £1,000 from my younger son to enable me to live until the proceeds came through. I had no option other than to rent but by doing so I was able to live and have savings to live on.

My health has suffered over the past twenty years due to the amount of hours I worked every day and the stress my body has been through.

My body is worn out, my joints ache, I have fybromyalgia and pernicious anaemia, both of which cause extreme tiredness. I can't stand for too long nor sit for too long or else I stiffen up. I would find it hard working a 9-5 day. I do my housework in a fashion, I stop and start, do a little, sit and have a rest then start again. It has been known for me to hoover the bedroom and have a sleep, on the bed, in the middle of doing so.

Then I can get up and continue where I left off. I am just grateful I have my money from my home to live on.

I rented the property, to allow myself to pay off the lifetime mortgage. I would say to anyone, think twice before you commit to anything like this, as it cost me fifteen thousand pounds interest in five years.

I used to worry that I would outlive my savings but now I give all my worries up to God, I know he provides. I hear and follow his guidance. It has gotten me the perfect home. I have cut down on my living costs and I try not to waste money but respect it and the luxuries it provides for me.

If you are struggling financially, start by examining where you spend your money and how could you possibly cut back. Instead of spending, use what you have, whether it be food in the freezer, clothes hanging in your wardrobe, enjoy the furniture, ornaments, bedding you have already and do what you can to make things stretch. Cook a meal instead of going out for one, don't go out if you can't afford to. Have friends round, cook a meal and buy some drink, watch a DVD rather than go to the cinema, it works out so much cheaper. Stop buying presents you don't need to. It's only the retailer who is better off. Openly tell your friends you are cutting back and can't afford to do certain things.

I was in quite a dark place one day and I needed to do exactly those things. There's nothing to be ashamed of. Quite possibly your friends could be quite pleased you have openly spoken about it, as they could well be struggling too.

Do not try and keep up with the Jones, as they say, don't try to impress. You do not know what others have, whether they are up to their eyes in debt but still drive a flash car and live in a fancy house.

Do a reality check, be you, and nobody else. If people around you don't like it, then they weren't worth knowing. Surround yourself with genuine people, people who love and respect you for who you are. Live within your means. You will see, you will end up living a much happier and peaceful life.

I have no worries or at least if there is something that is niggling away at me, I give it up to the Higher Force, that is. They have a much better solution than I could ever have.

Love yourself and everyone will love you. Small miracles do happen, be grateful and enjoy this precious life you have been given, the natural beauty you have around you, it costs nothing. Please take one day at a time, as I said, small miracles do happen.

And remember a positive mind will give you a positive life.

Do You Ever Feel Lost?

Do you ever feel lost or at least feel you have lost your way in life?

You don't know what you are meant to be doing?

Not sure if you should be somewhere else?

What is the meaning of your life?

Why have you been put on this earth?

What job are you meant to be doing?

So many questions! That is very much how I was feeling one day. I seemed to have lost my way and needed someone to give me directions.

It's a strange feeling, amplified by the fact I had been reading a book by Cecelia Ahern called A Place Called Here. It was about where do missing people and items disappear to? Maybe it's making me question where I should be.

Like you, I still have an off day which I have to turn around.

The Merry Month Of May

Oh, isn't it lovely when the sun comes out. May and I had been told that the temperatures were on the up! So I was very brave and discarded my winter coat. Mind you I still had my leggings, jumper and scarf on. It is definitely far too early to reveal the whiter than white legs.

As the saying goes, 'Don't cast a clout until May's out.' It was beautiful walking with Alfie through the woodland, he must have been enjoying it to, as he didn't seem to want to go back home and so we found a park bench and sat down.

Alfie, sitting on the bench too, he refuses to sit on the ground, I think he thinks he is human. We sat there enjoying the peace and tranquility, the only sounds I could hear were the birdsong, the crows high up in the trees and the church clock chiming in the distance.

When we had had enough, we ventured further into the woodland. I noticed the leaves had started to burst open with the warmth of the sun. The sun had also encouraged the wild garlic to flower along with the bluebells and forget-me-nots.

I got a lot of pleasure admiring everyone's garden on my way home. You see I don't have a garden but I don't feel bereft, as I don't have all the hard work which comes with a garden but what I can do is enjoy everyone else's garden. The colours of the spring flowers, so vibrant and the blossom on the trees making everywhere look so beautiful.

I just love this time of year. It is so uplifting and it makes my heart sing, just like the birds. I noticed a different bird up on one of the branches today, it was black and had white stripes on it's head with a spot of red. I looked it up when I got home, it was a bullfinch.

After I returned home, I decided to sit at my small bistro table, which I have on the small patio area outside of my lounge window. I had taken my jotter and pen out with me, as I had felt in the mood to write. I might as well enjoy the best of the day. I quite enjoy sitting here, as it is open to the private roadway which passes by my house, people walk up and down it all day. They stop and have a chat or just say hi, as they pass by.

It made me think, as I sat there, how we connect with some people and yet others, we don't seem to engage with at all. It is said that every person is in our lives for a reason, maybe to teach us a lesson or to enrich our lives.

A lady I know from church stopped to have a chat, she lives in a very large, old house, just a few hundred metres from where I live. She said she envied me my little courtyard/patio, as it is a rather sociable spot. Whereas, she has a very large back garden, where she sometimes sits but gets very lonely, as she sees no-one. When she had left, I gave thanks for my little spot with my pots and table and two chairs, it certainly is a very sociable spot. It gets the sun for most of the day and I never feel lonely when I sit there. I am very grateful I have it.

Living The Dream

Have you ever had a dream of doing something big but everyone tried to tell you it was too big and you would never succeed at it?

Well yesterday my elder son text me six photos of a warehouse. He had gone to view a very large warehouse, in the hope that he could start his own business.

I panicked! I am sorry to say, I thought it was just too big and I actually said "Could you not do it on a smaller scale?"

I was really in fear mode. I even went to the lengths of texting his younger brother, Paul, asking if he would go and talk some sense into Steven.

Well I was walking home from the gym and suddenly I remembered my mum saying; "You'll never do it!" to anything and everything I dreamed of doing.

Looking back it actually had the opposite effect of knocking my confidence, it actually put fire in my belly and made me more determined that I would succeed and I always did.

The job I would never get…..I did. The painting she swore down I hadn't painted…..I had and it is hanging in pride of place on my lounge wall. The business everyone said my ex husband and I could not make a go of……was very successful for fourteen years until our marriage ended and the business had to be sold.

So who was I to say my son's dream would not be a success!

I texted him in Dubai and told him that I would be the proudest mum alive to see his business succeed and I gave him my blessings.

He did however choose to rent a space in a premises from a friend. So much more sensible but it was his choice not mine, with maybe just a little guidance.

Who are we to stop other people living their dream. We can only offer them our love, support, guidance and very best wishes and pray that they will succeed in whatever they choose to do.

It's A Small World

I was waiting to catch a bus one day and a little old lady with a dog and a shopping trolley dismounted from a bus, which had just pulled into the bus stop, from further up the Dale.

We got talking and she said she had a caravan at Cowshill and had to catch four buses to get her home. She lived three miles outside of Sunderland but she didn't mind, as it was a ride out. The bus arrived and we got on and she came to sit beside me.

I asked her "Whereabouts in Sunderland do you live? I used to live three miles outside of Sunderland."

She said "At the Board Inn."

To which I replied "So did I!"

Curiosity was killing me, so I asked her "Just whereabouts in Herrington do you live?"

She said "Balmoral Terrace."

To which I replied "My mum lived there."

She said "Are you a Norman?"

I replied "Yes I was."

To which she replied "I used to go to school with your brother!"

Then she went on to tell me that she could remember me passing by her house with my mum in my car.

We carried on talking and she told me it was her husband's birthday and how the house she lived in had become too big for them. I told her that a friend of mine was looking for a bungalow and she could well be interested. I would let my friend know when I got back home and if she was interested, I would tell her to get in touch.

By this time, my stop was approaching and so I bid her farewell and said it had been good to talk to her.

I was so excited, I went home, rang my friend, told her the tale and she said she would go and pop a note in the lady's letterbox that very afternoon.

I thought wouldn't it be funny if I had managed to find my friend a home, when here I am twenty six miles away in Weardale.

It certainly is a small world!

Driving = Freedom

I mentioned earlier that due to health problems I had been unable to drive for six weeks.

Well I had been given permission to drive again. Today was the day that I could get back behind the wheel and how fantastic it felt. I only drove six miles up the Dale, to go a message and to take Alfie for a walk along by the river bank.

I had never felt more grateful in my life. Getting my independence back but also I could now empathise with others who were in a similar situation.

I had often sat during the cold winter months, gazing out at my little car, thinking I walk to most places, should I maybe sell it?

Well I was well and truly put to the test and the answer is NO!

I am very grateful that I have the ability to be able to drive a car and so, so grateful I possess one. I will never question it again.

Holidays

Don't you just love them! But, are you like me, as the time to leave gets closer, you panic. What on earth do you pack? You check the weather reports. Oh no! You see showers forecast, great, that means an umbrella will have to go in. Yes, and you had better take a raincoat.

You notice that it would be cooler at night, okay so you had better put a cardigan/jacket in. Will you be going out and about on trips? Yes, well that means comfortable shoes, walking shoes, a hat in case it is too hot, don't want sunstroke. Oh yes and you'll need sunglasses and suncream. Better pack after sun just in case you overdo it.

Then there's Imodium for the funny tummy, antihistamines just in case of an allergic reaction, mosquito spray, headache tablets. you nearly forgot, a few plasters, just in case of blisters.

You haven't even started on the clothes! I don't know about you but I start with the shoes, they've got to be comfy ones and allow for the fact that my feet swell in the aeroplane never mind the heat.

I learnt this from a very early holiday, I must say, I was pregnant at the time but I had packed all of my glamorous unpractical shoes and unfortunately flight socks had not been invented then. Hence I got off the plane with two tree trunks for legs and no ankles! My first job was to buy a pair of flip flops which I wore for the duration of my holiday. Yes we learn the hard way, don't we!

Now the clothes, after looking at so many holiday snaps and thinking 'My goodness did you really go out looking like that!' I have now banned shorts from the case. I now pack sundresses, which I must say, if you, like me, have not got that perfect figure, a sundress hides a multitude of sins. Underwear and pjs next, dressing gown in case you have to evacuate (I have had to a couple of times in the past), swimming costume, wrap, phone adapter, plug, hot air brush, can't survive without it. A towel and hairdryer, if not provided.

So you have got the daywear sorted, all you need now is for the evenings. A light pair of trousers with a jacket to match, to keep the mozzies from attacking. A couple of long T-Shirtie type dresses, smart and comfortable and a couple of dresses just in case you get to go somewhere special. An evening bag, well not as such, I should have said a small bag which will go with all outfits, a beach bag, a little bit of jewellery, again which will go with everything and you are just about there.

You heave a sigh of relief as you stand on the scales with your case in your hand, just about collapsing, yes, it's under the required weight, just! Now all there is to do, is the hand luggage. Well saying that I forgot to mention to put your toiletries in. You put them in the case then re-check the scales.

If you are like me, I keep a toilet bag ready, just in case. It saves so much time if you are going away for a weekend, rushed into hospital, or going on holiday. I keep it up to date at all times.

So all you need now is your passport, make-up, foreign money, insurance document, a good book/magazine, some mints.

I personally always carry mints with me when I am travelling just in case I get delayed then I have something to keep me going.

A wrap in case the air-con on the plane is turned up too high plus it doubles up if it gets chilly on an evening whilst you are away, then I think you are there. Brilliant, all set and ready to go.

Just need to do Domestos down the loo and sinks, check everywhere is spic and span, bed changed for when you get back, dishcloth steeping in Domestos and boiling water. One last check, everything switched off, nothing going to go bad in the fridge and all the rubbish has gone out. Just need to lock up and then you are off! Drop the dog off at the dog minders, that's if you have one.

PHEW! Exhausted! You need a holiday!!!

The Airport

You have arrived at the airport, you are on time, you weren't held up in traffic and you didn't get a puncture, great! You only have to check in and my goodness do you hope your bathroom scales were weighing correctly.

One of the ground crew for the airline calls you forward, requesting your passport and E ticket, "Have you packed your luggage yourself and have you been asked to carry anything for anyone else?" he/she asks.

"Yes and no!" you reply. That is fine, can you now put your luggage on the conveyor belt to be weighed. You stand there holding your breath, as the numbers on the screen in front of the desk start to go up. Fantastic, you have 2 kilos to spare! You have forgotten to start breathing again. Breathe!!!

You stand there, your mind ticking over, by the time you use all of the toiletries and leave behind the ones with just a little bit in the bottles, you will have space and kilos spare to buy something! Oh yes, you have to have a memento of where you have been, a fridge magnet, a new bag, shoes, something from the local market, just something!

I must say at this point, my best buy was a pair of white cotton cropped trousers, bought for 3 euros, at the Saturday Market in Barga, Tuscany, what a bargain!

Okay, sorry I was getting excited about spare kilos. So what must you do now? A quick check to make sure everyone is booked in. Your party all agree that a bacon butty and a cup of coffee is called for, even though you have just had your breakfast two hours ago.

"Well, what are you going on about? You are on your holidays!" I am sure you will hear that phrase many more times for the duration of your holiday.

You have de-stressed whilst enjoying your bacon butty and coffee but now it is time to go upstairs and go through security.

"Please remove your coats, shoes, belts, watches and please put lap tops, phones, and keys in a separate tray. Liquids under 100ml in a sealed plastic bag also in a tray." Yes, you have done all that, you wait to go through the scanner, it's now your turn. It bleeps! Shucks, what have you left on?

"Can you please take off your jewellery and put it in the tray?" Try again, again it beeps, you go through but not before she has frisked you.

I think it's my underwired bra that does it.

Once through, you collect all of your gear and try and find a quiet spot where you can go and dress yourself again. Why did you get dressed to come to the airport in the first place? You might as well have come in your pjs and dressed in the toilets once you were safely through security.

Everyone is now stressed again, due to the ordeal of security and the possibility that someone has left something behind in a tray. Time for a drink, you certainly need one now.

It is one of the most stressful things you have to go through but the end result is so worthwhile. A visit to the bar, a stiff drink to calm the nerves or a coffee, as you sit and wait for your flight to be called. Or if you are a lady then you find a comfy seat, deposit your hand luggage with a willing member of your party with whom you are travelling with, then oh, you think it is time for maybe a little retail therapy or maybe a manicure if you haven't had time for one before you left home.

As time goes by the tension/excitement is growing. Is the flight on time? Is it delayed? Has it come up yet on the screen? What gate have you got to go to? If you have returned to your seat to wait, you have a look around, has anyone got the same ticket on their luggage? You sit and surmise who may be on your flight.

Your flight comes up, you see a major shift, people are gathering their hand luggage, children, buggies etc. and they start heading towards the stairway which leads to the departure gates. Well you would think it was the start of the January sales, everyone is rushing, as if there is an urgency for them to get where they are going. What for you might ask? Just to sit and wait again until your flight is called ready for you to embark.

You have your passport in hand, you check your ticket to see which seat you have been allocated. Are you at the front, middle or back of the plane? Will they call you first? Oh no! They are calling in reverse order, panic! You will be getting on last and now you are wondering if there will be any space left to put your hand luggage in the overhead locker or will you have to store it under the seat in front of you?

At last you are called. You either get on a bus or walk to the plane, the air hostess welcomes you on board as you step on to the plane and directs you to where your seat has been allocated. You put your luggage away, get out a drink, book/magazine and tuck it all into the pocket in front of you, you sit down, fasten your seat belt and sigh.

You turn to the person next to you and say hi, that is if it isn't one of your fellow passengers and then settle down, looking at the duty free, what snacks are available in flight and which films are available to watch. Time to relax, there is nothing more you can do, you are ready to start your holiday!

I must say, these days, I do either use a four wheeled piece of hand luggage, which is so much easier to drag round with me or if I am being very minimalistic I only take a handbag on board, with my book inside and I have a scarf/shawl around my shoulders just in case I am cold during the flight. I leave my jewellery in my handbag until I have got through security and wear easy to take off / put on shoes. If I am only taking hand luggage with me, I buy my toiletries in Boots, once I am in duty free, so that I have no problem with quantities. Anything for an easy life and to cut down on stress.

Happy holidays!

A Walk In The Woods

It was a cool, dull, calm day in May, we had had sun for quite a few days now but today by 11:00 am, there was a 40% chance of rain. I thought I had better get a spurt on and take Alfie for his morning walk.

With the forecast not looking good, I looked out of my kitchen window and noticed a lady with a headscarf on, passing by my window. I decided I had better put a warmer coat on and preferably one with a hood. So dressed for warmth and possibly a shower, Alfie and I set off.

Actually, I am never quite sure where we are going for our walk, as Alfie takes the lead, literally. If I try to take him somewhere he doesn't want to go, he stops and won't budge. He looks at me, then looks in the direction he wants to go. Liking an easy, peaceful life, I give in and let him guide me. He seems to know every nook, cranny, and short cut in the town.

We set off and he decided to take a right turn and go down a gravel path to the nearby caravan site, which overlooks the River Wear. It's very picturesque and a very popular walk since the town received a lottery grant enabling them to make it wheelchair friendly.

I passed an old school friend who informed me that he had just put some weed and feed on his lawn and he was hoping it would rain, as it needed watering in. So I said, "It's you who we have to blame for the change in the weather, is it?"

I carried on my way, through the turnstile gate and along the pathway. I noticed some orange poppies flowering beside some bluebells and thought how inspiring nature is. I am sure designers in the textile industry must get a lot of inspiration from nature.

Even though it was cool, Alfie stopped at his favourite seat to rest for a while. It was whilst we were sitting down and I was daydreaming, that I noticed how still everything was. There was no noise of children throwing stones into the river, no dogs barking, waiting for their owners to throw sticks or balls for them. It was peace, perfect peace, even the birds had stopped singing. It was so tranquil.

Suddenly I was jolted back to the present, Alfie had spotted a dog, a rather large one, at that. He decided to get the first bark in, letting the other dog know he was not a dog to be messed with. I think it's called small dog syndrome.

Peace disturbed, we got up and went on our way. As we passed the field with the sheep and lambs in it, I noticed even the lambs were huddled close to their mothers in the corner of the field, barring one. This lamb was laid with his back to the others, at the other side of the field. I wondered if it had been 'Sent to Coventry' so to speak, by the others or was it the case that it felt it was too superior to be with the rest of them.

Do animals have an hierarchy? I do know I have a friend with alpacas and the ginger one gets bullied plus the other alpacas pinch his food. So it's not just humans. If you are different in any way, you are left on the outside, sad really as this should not be. God created us all perfect.

I could smell the wild garlic and I noticed the creepers wrapped around the trunks of the trees had been cut. I had earlier seen a dipper, on a stone in the river, bobbing up and down looking for his lunch.

It was so beautiful and energising in the woodland, so much so today with no-one about. Everyone must be indoors, catching up on housework or jobs that needed doing. They really didn't know what they were missing.

As I came out of the woodland, I noticed about six baby bunnies enjoying their freedom on the football pitch in the recreation ground. I also noticed the moles had also been very busy. They must have been big ones, if the mole hills were anything to go by.

Alfie seemed tired this morning, as he was walking slowly and kept stopping for a breather. I didn't mind, as it gave me time to notice my surroundings, like the purple lilac tree. I just had to stop, gently get hold of one of it's flowers and inhale the beautiful fragrance. It took me back to my childhood and the lilac trees dad had planted in our garden. Dad loved his lilac trees, only ours had had white flowers on them but the fragrance was just as powerful.

As I approached home, I thought it was time for coffee and half an hour reading my book before I started on the jobs waiting patiently to be done.

It's all about balance you know.

Why?

Why do I worry about what others think?
Why do I worry about the future?
Why have I been ill so many times in my life?
Why do I worry about my sons?

I kept telling myself I didn't need to worry because I couldn't see the bigger picture and I just knew it would all be okay in the end.

I do believe our life is like a jigsaw, the jigsaw has been done in advance, the only thing is we can't see the finished product. At certain times of my life I felt I had been given a few pieces of the jigsaw all at once, which quickly fitted together giving me an insight of why things had happened the way they had. Now when I look back over my life I think, well if that hadn't happened I couldn't have experienced this or that. I do find it fascinating as I get older.

I have wasted so much time feeling low and being ill, in hindsight I think I've been grieving for my mum, life has been passing me by. The fear of doing things. Since mum died I seemed to have gone into a decline, I think it's because the buck stops with me now. The last of the older generation has gone. My dad died at the age of sixty two when I was only twenty seven and my elder brother died fifteen years ago.

It feels weird and quite scary because I am that generation now. I used to think it was strange when I heard older people say they were an orphan, as they had lost their parents but I understand now. I keep telling myself I am never alone, I must say at this point, Steven went to Dubai New Year's Day, mum died 6th February and Paul my younger son moved to Dubai 29th August all in 2014. The Universe was clearing my life for something special.

I have God and I am surrounded with angels protecting and guiding me. My family wouldn't want me sitting mourning and moping after them and watching everyone else getting on with their lives. They would want me to get on with my life.

So I made a promise to myself, to get the best out of every day. Immediately after I thought this, the sun came out and shone down on me. Could that have been a sign that I had eventually seen the light. I made a decision that I was not going to wait around for anyone, I was just going to get on with living.

I didn't need to climb Everest but what I did realise was that I love to write and travel. My friends think I am strange as I get excited over a new notepad or pen, mind you the pen has to be a fine writer, I am very fussy when it comes to my tools.

No, I didn't want to sit at a computer all day typing or dictating. I just love to see the pen flow over the paper. I have done, since I learnt to write all those years ago, as a child. I would sit and practice my handwriting until it was as neat as I could possibly get it.

I would save up my pocket money, then when I had enough, I would get the bus into Sunderland and go to Hills, the bookshop and buy stationary, pens and books to read. I guess these were and still are my passion, well alongside clothes, shoes and bags!

Moods

Have you ever noticed how you dress and how you go for different colours, depending on what mood you are in.

If you are feeling happy you will tend to go for bright colours but if you are feeling low then you are likely to choose black, navy or grey.

This was brought to my attention one day in church, I had been going through a tough time when I was getting divorced and unknowingly I always wore black, navy and grey. Then one day I went to church with a fuchsia pink jumper on and an old lady in the congregation came over to me to say, it was lovely to see me wearing a bright colour.

I was amazed, it had never struck me that I had been constantly wearing dark colours, but others obviously had noticed!

Now I love bright clothes and if I do wear black, navy or grey, I tend to wear a bright scarf or colourful shoes and matching bag to brighten the outfit.

Update

I started writing this book in 2016, it had been a tough year. I was shocked when I realised that pneumonia holistically meant 'You have lost the will to live!'

It hit home like a bolt of lightening, as when I was in Dubai in December 2015 for Steven's 29th birthday, I realised that both my boys had settled very well into Dubai life. They had their own lives. I was redundant, I wasn't needed anymore!

I actually only saw Steven on three occasions whilst I was there as his work commitment was unbelievable. He was working 12 hours every day and his holiday which he had planned for me going out there, had been cancelled.

As Steven was taking me back to Paul's house on my last night before I left, he said to me, "Ahhh mum you aren't leaving already?"

These words haunt me!

The Queen's 90th Birthday

The Queen's 90th birthday was coming up and when the President of our local W.I. asked if anyone on the committee (yes I was on it!) was willing to organise a party to celebrate the occasion, there wasn't a twitter!

I was still recovering from being poorly and so I sat and didn't utter a word, avoiding all eye contact. My friend, Madam President was very good at giving me the eye.

Well I got home and on the evening I sat and thought about it, my conscience was pricking me. I knew I could quite easily organise it. I put pen to paper and by bedtime I had more or less sorted it all out.

We would have a proper English afternoon tea, with a singer for the entertainment. I ordered Union Jack serviettes, table confetti consisting of crowns and clear, blue and red crystals, nothing tacky and we would get a local caterer to cater, allowing all of us time to enjoy the afternoon. I applied for a grant from our local Weardale Action Group, which they very kindly agreed to and by the next meeting it was all sorted.

The day was actually a huge success, the room was filled to capacity, everyone dressed in red, white and blue. It was a very memorable occasion and well worth the effort.

Lesson; Don't sit back, if you think you are capable of doing the task in hand. Speak up and volunteer!

The Black Hole

Do we ever realise we are sinking into a black hole or maybe just into a place we would prefer not to be in? I only realised this one day when I went to wash the dishes that were waiting by the sink, three days worth, patiently waiting for me to be in a better place, making me aware that they were still there.

I hadn't been very well at all that week, in fact I hadn't been well for six months. I seemed to have got one thing after another. I could count on one hand the number of weeks I had actually felt well. But this particular week I wasn't in a very good place. Was it because when I looked in the mirror I didn't like what I saw?

My eyes and my face were really sore and swollen, my skin had broken out and it felt and looked as if I had had acid poured over it, even my lips were all swollen and sore. I felt drained of energy and it took me all of my time to drag myself out of bed on a morning.

I think if it hadn't been for Alfie needing to go for his walk I could have quite easily stayed in bed for the day.

I had visited the dentist, my teeth were troubling me and my dentist thought I had an abscess coming. I had also gone to the local A & E about my face, then two days later I visited my G.P. I was on antibiotics and I had been given antibiotic eye cream. Not Good!

A few days later I woke in a much better place, I felt more like myself and when I looked into the mirror, I actually looked like me. As I went walking, I stopped to smell the roses, smiled whilst watching the bunnies running about, sat and watched the birds in flight. I was so thankful to be alive, to enjoy the wonders of nature. To be able to have my sight and to see everything, my hearing to enjoy the bird song, having the ability to walk, touch and smell. My heart was singing with gladness.

Nothing I was experiencing cost anything, it just took the time to notice what was around me. I felt the luckiest person alive. I chattered to my old school friend who has a caravan on the site I walk through.

I then took Alfie, who was quite tired by now, home and I went off to the local butchers to buy some fresh chicken. I had just reached the door to the butchers when I spotted two friends, each one coming from a different direction. I explained I must go in to John, the butchers before he closed. They invited me to join them for coffee/lunch, whatever I fancied. I enthusiastically accepted.

I thoroughly enjoyed a good catch up over poached eggs on toast washed down with a cup of decaf coffee. Then it was time to leave, I said my farewells then made my way home. My day was proving to be a good one.

When I got back, I put the chicken in the oven, put my meditation CD on and meditated for a while. I had planned to go to the cinema but I decided to stay in and do my housework, lifting my spirits even more.

Remember, tomorrow is another day and hopefully you will feel so much better, don't give up, have faith.

What Me Wear Today?

Are you interested in clothes? Apparently as soon as I was able to string a sentence together my mum said that the first thing I would say when I woke up and what is so strange is it's the first think I still think about even to this day is, what shall I wear today?

I might think about my shoes first, do they have to be practical, comfortable or am I going somewhere special that I need to get a pair of best shoes out for an airing.

Then I will get up and look out of the window to see what the weather is doing. Is it hot / cold / sunny / cloudy / wet / dry? So many things to consider before I can decide what to put on. After deciding whether it has to be trousers & top or a dress, then I have to decide what underwear to go under what I have chosen.
Finally is it a scarf or jewellery to finish off the outfit or both.

I have to say I am not so bothered about the jewellery as I am a scarf person. I just love scarves, so much so, I must have over sixty in my collection, lightweight, silky and thick chunky ones for the colder days, all of them in a variety of colours.

At one time I always wore jewellery but as I get older I feel a scarf distracts from my not so slim waist and ageing neck. A scarf can always uplift and complete an outfit don't you think?

All done, I take a glance in my full length mirror, tell myself I love you! Well there's no-one else here to tell me! I give myself the seal of approval before stepping outside my bedroom and ready to face the world.

Every day look in the mirror and tell yourself you love you! One day you will believe it.

Fear, Feeling Lost And Lonely

I'd had a pretty tough week and after crying for two days I decided it was time to sit and talk to God, offload my fears, worries and regrets and give it all up to the Higher Realms.

I sat and poured out my heart then sat in silence for a while, with just the flame of a candle flickering. A beautiful warm feeling crept over me and my heart felt light and loved. I was at peace.

The next morning I woke feeling so much more positive and ready to get on with my life. I went to church and the sermon was all about giving up our troubles to God. I would say that was confirmation!

God does not want us to be troubled, he wants us to be at peace. He is there to carry us when the going gets tough. It's just like that poem 'Footsteps in the sand.' I just love that poem.

Remember F E A R stands for False Evidence Appearing Real!
Don't let it rule your life, there is a bigger picture which we can't see.

Bank Holiday Weekends

I may have already mentioned earlier that this is one of my pet hates. For anyone living on their own, having no partner, their children have moved away, you will know exactly what I mean when I say "I hate Bank Holiday Weekends," I feel like Billy No Mates. Everyone is out and about with their loved ones and families.

I was very grateful one Bank Holiday Weekend when a friend asked if I would like to go to a Best of British Fair, in the grounds of Bishop Auckland Castle. The castle would also be open to allow the general public to see the stunning Spanish collection of paintings on display. I was delighted, brilliant, I thought, that was the Saturday taken care of.

Then I got a phone call from another friend saying she and her husband would like to take me out on the Sunday for lunch, as she knew how much I disliked Bank Holidays. So thoughtful and I am so fortunate to have Gill and Roy as my friends, I couldn't believe it, that was the Sunday taken care of.

Well I couldn't believe my luck when on the Sunday evening another friend, Debs WhatsApp me, saying she was coming to see me on the Monday and would I like to go out for lunch.

Wow! My prayers had well and truly been answered. I can't tell you how grateful I was. I am so grateful for my amazing set of friends.

Thank you Lord.

Review Your Journey

I was feeling overwhelmed one morning, the Universe had given me an insight into my life and I realised I was not on my own at all.

That very same day an old friend came to have lunch with me and stayed until 5:00 p.m. Then my next door neighbour popped in for a chat. She had just left when another friend text "Could she pop over?" My day had been full of laughter, reminiscing and plans for the future.

One thing I had thought about when I was reminiscing was, how much guts it had taken for me to go off on my own to South Africa to do a painting course with Hazel Soan in 2008, just after my divorce. I was very much an amateur artist and yet there I was, thousands of miles away from home, on my own, sharing a room with a complete stranger. I was truly out of my comfort zone, trying to paint various subjects on different locations and I thoroughly enjoyed every minute of the ten days I was out there. I must remember if I can do that then there are lots of other things waiting for me to do.

It turned out to be one of my most memorable holidays. When I look at those paintings now I realise just how good they are, well in my opinion they are and to be honest my opinion is the only one that counts.

I had only booked it because, I had been very ill with unstable angina and then my lower back had gone into spasm and I had been bed ridden. I got the email advertising the holiday and thought, that's it, that's my carrot. If I book it I have something to work towards and sometimes that is all we need, a carrot, something to work towards, keeping us focused and taking just one step at a time to reach our goal but one day you will do it. You will look back and think it was so much easier than what you had ever thought possible.

Before I went to bed that night I went on to Facebook and Doreen Virtue had posted the card of the day 'Review and Contemplate,' meaning - you've accomplished a great deal in your life and you have much to be proud of.

Look back on your life and you will be surprised just what you have overcome and achieved. Then decide what your next challenge will be. It doesn't have to be a great adventure, it could be just facing your fear of the dark, yes something as simple as that, which prevents you from doing so much. Instead of focusing on what it will take to achieve your goal just plod along at your own pace. Okay some days it might feel you have slid back a step or two but focus on the now and just keep going. You can and will do it.

When you contemplate on the past, then the present, the future becomes clearer. What is your Divine Life Purpose? Don't be distracted by conventional thinking, be the real you.

Overwhelmed!

There's no other word for it. I was sorting out the last of my boxes from moving house almost three years ago. There were three rather large black boxes, full to the brim of painting gear, not to paint the walls with. No!

There were acrylics, crayons, pencils, watercolour paints, so much, that it covered the kitchen table, the benches and the floor.

I stood and looked at it all and I asked myself, "Who was this person that had purchased all of this stuff?"

No wonder I couldn't find the real me! Where was I? Why on earth had I bought all these painting materials, most of them unused.

There wasn't just the paints, there were fourteen palettes, over a hundred tubes of acrylic paints and possibly the same in watercolours. There were oils, charcoal, pencils, rubbers, bag of sponges, fifteen acrylic pads and about the same of watercolour pads and so many brushes of all shapes, sizes and usage.

I couldn't do anything other than stand and look at them. I literally was so overwhelmed, so much so, I left them cluttering my kitchen overnight. I just didn't know what to do with it all.

The next day when I got up and walked into the kitchen, I sat down and cried for the person who had bought all of this stuff. What on earth was I thinking of, to go out and buy all these things when 1 palette, 1 paintbox and several brushes and a pad of paper would have sufficed.

I went and had lunch with a friend and then came home revitalised and ready to tackle it all. I slowly went through everything, one pile at a time. I made a pile of what I actually needed and gave the rest to the charity, Age UK for a painting class for the aged. I hoped that some old people who couldn't afford materials but loved to paint as a hobby, would be able to do so and get some enjoyment out of it all.

The coloured pencils and sketch pads went to the children next door for their art classes. Everything was put to good use.

The thought for today :- Whatever you do, when you are out shopping, STOP! Think do you really need the item you are contemplating buying?

Also all of those things that you have bought, maybe for a hobby but are lying dormant in a box, could someone else be getting pleasure from using them, if you are not!

Possessions

Why do we buy so many clothes, books, magazines, ornaments, toys for our children, food which stays in the cupboard / fridge then gets tossed out because it is 'out of date'?

We collect, save, store, hoard, but why? It only blocks our lives.

God gave us these things, we must give thanks for them, be grateful and if we don't use them then we must pass them on to someone else, who will use them and get pleasure from them.

You will feel lighter, have more energy, you will be able to think clearer, your house won't be as cluttered, it will be easier to keep clean and it won't get so dusty and you can enjoy being in your home without loads of jobs staring you in the face, waiting to be done.

Lesson: You can appreciate just what you have, but always, whatever, be grateful at all times and give thanks.

When life gives you lemons, make lemonade.

Don't cry over the past, it's gone! You can't do anything about it.

Don't stress about the future, it hasn't arrived. Tomorrow will look after itself, so don't worry.

Live in the present and make each moment beautiful. Today is here to enjoy, live it as if it is your last.

Number 10

No I don't mean 10, Downing Street, I mean the coffee shop in our town (I call it a village). Alfie was at the dog sitters for the weekend, as I was due to go away but in the end it was cancelled. I decided to take him anyway, as I felt I needed some 'me' time. Silly really, you would think I was talking about a man, wouldn't you? But honestly you would think he was one, I get the look from him when I get ready to go out, you know the one I mean, the 'Not again' look.

Well anyway, when I had woken up I looked out of the window to see a beautiful sunny day. I decided to treat myself to a fried egg sandwich and a mug of weak black coffee. (The man on the T.V. said that fried eggs are more slimming than a bacon sandwich and I believe him, thousands wouldn't!) I took my book with me, a real treat!

I even dressed for summer, white cotton short skirt, a navy sleeveless T-shirt and a bonny three quarter sleeved navy, white, pink and lime green cardigan. I assure you it is much nicer than what it sounds like. All I needed were my sunglasses and then I looked the part. Off I went, sat down at one of the bistro tables outside on the pavement of No.10 and waited to be served.

I wasn't there two minutes before three ladies from church came and sat at the next table. We made polite conversation as I sat waiting for my sandwich and coffee to arrive. Then another couple from church stopped to talk to us, as they were passing by. It was literally only minutes before another lady I talk to, from church, stopped to ask how I was and then asked me about my book which was lying on the table.

She asked if she could join me for a coffee and before long, we had another two ladies join us. One I always say "Good morning" to and the other I go to the Knit and Natter Group with on a Wednesday afternoon.

The morning flew by and I happened to comment that I hadn't even read one page of my book. I was told, "You can read anytime!"

Of course they were right. When I went home I wouldn't have the wonderful company I had had all morning. Before I left, another table beside me filled with friends.

I needed to go home, the wet fish I had bought at John's, our local butchers, on my way to No.10, would be cooked if I stayed any longer. I thanked them for their company and said farewell.

I went home feeling very grateful for village life. I may live on my own but company is only five minutes walk away at No.10.

Toxic Relationships

Have you ever had a friend who seems to drain you of energy? It could even be a relative. By the time you say bye you feel drained and exhausted.

They come and sit down and tell you all of their troubles, ask for your advice but they never even think to say "How are you? What's been happening in your life?"

If you can connect with anyone in your life like this, if your relationship has gone off the boil, so to speak, they've outstayed their welcome. Then be kind to yourself and move on, time for a clear out. Don't feel, well I've known them a lifetime. Honestly, they have passed their sell by date.

Say goodbye to drama, toxic people and self criticism. Say yes to more happiness and love in your life. Time with good friends.

Money

Money is good it helps me to live a comfortable life.

Money is good when I can give it away to help others.

Money is very welcome, it enables me to pay my bills.

Money is great, as it has shown me what I can do with it.

Money is brilliant, it has given me my independence.

I have lived my life fully because money is there to allow me to do so.

Money is something that if I give it away I end up having more.

Money is really welcome especially when it can be saved.

Money is a way of helping me to live my dreams.

Money is helping me to travel and see the world.

With money I am financially secure, with money to spare and share.

<u>BUT</u>

Money is not to be worshipped as it is not a god.

Neither is it something that you should let rule your life.

It is something we need to survive but don't let it be the 'be all and end all' in life.

There are so many wonderful things that don't cost anything, we just need time to appreciate them.

PART TWO

In the second part of my book I hope that if you have lost someone close to you it will give you a little comfort and hope. It may even give you a different perspective of looking at life and death. Or maybe it will just show you that when your life is well and truly falling apart, you can see good coming out of it, you just maybe have to look that little bit harder. I hope it helps.

Every Step Unfolds The Next Step Of Our Journey

It was the early hours of Saturday, the 6th August 2016 I had been sitting up late, watching the opening ceremony of the 2016 Olympics when I realised I must have nodded off because I suddenly woke up to see that it was 2:30 a.m. and way past my bedtime. I dragged myself off the settee and took myself off to bed.

I wasn't asleep twenty minutes when my mobile phone rang. It was my younger son Paul. I looked at my clock to see that it was 3:00 a.m. I automatically thought he must have been out with his friends nightclubbing, as he was in England working. He lives and normally works in Dubai, as does my elder son, Steven.

I answered the phone and what he told me, in fact I couldn't believe what he told me, I had to ask him to repeat what he said,

"Mam, Steven's dead!"

I started to cry, I became hysterical.

"Please don't cry mam." he said.

I asked the questions any mum would ask,

"Have you got someone with you? Are you ok?" I knew he wasn't but I had to ask all the same. Then I asked "How did Steven die?"

Steven had been riding his motor bike, on his way home after being out with his girlfriend and friends, when he was involved in a road incident. He had died instantly. He had broken his back, his neck and he had suffered a brain haemorrhage. His girlfriend had been travelling in her car, close behind and unfortunately had witnessed the incident.

My life changed forever that day, as did I. I will never be the same person again. A part of me died. My beautiful twenty nine year old son Steven, was dead.

Paul told me he was going to get a flight back to Dubai that morning and I could meet him back at his house. As soon as I got off the phone, I felt I had to confide in someone. Who could I ring? Most of my friends have partners and I didn't want to disturb them, so I decided to ring my friend Margaret, who although she lived twenty six miles away said she would come immediately.

My mind was in overdrive. I was crying so much, I was sitting, rocking my body back and forth. I felt physically sick, I had this huge lump in my throat that would not go. (It didn't for quite a long time afterwards, it still appears if something drastic happens.)

I could not believe this was happening to me but I had to try to make my mind accept what I had just heard and deal with what I had to do.

My next call was to Emirates to see if I could get booked on their lunchtime flight, flying from Newcastle to Dubai. I rang, explained the situation and they said there was only Business Class seats available, the cost for a return was £2,200.00. I think I asked him three times if there were any Economy seats but he said "No, we only have Business Class available."

I had to agree to the Business Class ticket, as I had to get to Dubai without delay and so I booked my ticket.

I then had to focus on packing a case, I have never packed so quickly nor so efficiently in all of my life, it just shows that when you have to, you can. I packed what I would normally use for a weekend case, with everything I thought I would need for a week.

The temperature in Dubai was averaging fifty two degrees centigrade, I can't normally stand it when it gets up into the late twenties but I knew I had to, I had to pull out all the stops and function. I also had to take into consideration that I would be dealing with the authorities, in a muslim country and so I would have to be covered up. I put in long dresses with a long black chiffon shirt, which I could use to cover my arms. I had to be respectful of their custom.

Paul rang back, he couldn't get hold of his dad, could I try? Well I must have tried about ten times, as did Paul, each time the phone would ring once, then go onto engaged.

(I realised later, that that's how it had to be, he hadn't to know until five hours later - everything is how it should be and when we understand this, we stop worrying.)

My friend arrived, more tears and tight comforting hugs. She wanted to know what she could do for me. I explained that I had booked myself a seat on the Emirates Dubai flight and I was busy packing my case. She went on to my computer to find out what one needed to do when a U.K. citizen dies in the United Arab Emirates.

It got to 8:0 a.m. and we still hadn't got in touch with the boys' dad, so my friend rang her daughter, who lived not too far away from where he lives and asked if she could go to his house and ask him to ring me, which she did. He rang me asking what did I want? When I told him, obviously he broke down.

My friend in the meantime wrote down the fourteen steps we needed to go through, once we had arrived in Dubai and all of the documents which were required from various authorities. Each document requiring a stamp by the authorities and a number of copies. Thirty two pages in total were needed before the authorities would release Steven's body and allow us to bring his remains out of Dubai.

Margaret tried to get me to eat, I felt so sickly I couldn't eat a thing, I had so much to think about and as time went by, I had to think of notifying family and friends that Steven had died, before I left the country.

A few friends came as soon as they heard, everyone was mortified, they didn't know what to say or do, it was so difficult.

Eventually it was time for my friend to kindly take me to the airport, which was an hour's drive away. When we got there, she gave me a great big hug as she dropped me off, said she was sorry she couldn't come with me and support me.

I tried to fight back the tears as I made my way inside the terminal to check in. The sooner I was in Dubai the better, all I wanted was to get there without the bother.

One of Paul's friends, I was told later, had gone to his dad's house to be with him and give him support. He apparently had gone on line and got an economy seat on the same flight as me, costing £780.00 for a return flight and then he had brought him to the airport.

After checking in, I proceeded through security. As I came through duty free I heard my name being called. There he was, the boys' dad, waiting for me. It wasn't easy, trying to cope with my son's death and having to be in close proximity with my ex of thirteen years.

I had to do this for Steven and Paul. We had a lot to get through this week and we had to try and co-operate. I sat down and we had a staggered conversation before our flight was called. I left him as we boarded the plane, found my seat and as I was waiting for the passengers to board, a gentleman looked at me and said "It can't be that bad!" If only he knew.

Never pass judgement on people, as you just do not know what they are dealing with in their lives.

We took off, I tried to watch a movie, I noticed the guy sitting in the seat to my left was watching Johnny Cash, one of Steven's favourite musicians. It made me think of him, I tried to keep composed. I couldn't eat any food, nothing would go down.

I suddenly thought, I had always hoped that I would one day get the opportunity to travel Business Class and I quietly thought to myself, if I had known my son would have to die, for me to be able to fly Business Class, then I would rather have never flown in Business Class at all. I truly felt sick inside at the very thought.

Be careful what you wish for and what you have to sacrifice for it to happen.

About three hours into the flight I started to cry, I was sobbing quietly. I was relieved the lights were low and nearly everyone was sleeping. The air hostess came to check if I was okay and I said no I wasn't! I felt as if I was having a sort of panic attack. It was so hard being surrounded by families and the majority of which were going on holiday, all happy whilst my world had fallen apart. I felt I wanted to scream.

I told Lauren, the air hostess, what had happened.

She asked "Would I like to talk about it?"

I replied "Yes I would."

She spent the next three and a half hours on her knees, at my side, talking to me and holding my hand. She was wonderful. She had just lost her nana in the February and so understood a little of what I was going through.

About forty five minutes before landing she asked me to go with her to the galley, as she was required to do some jobs and whilst she was busy she gave me an ice-cream. It was quite refreshing as my throat felt terrible. I stayed there until it was time to land, when I had to return to my seat.

The steward brought my 'ex' up to Business Class, so that we could both get priority disembarkation. We would have to go through security before collecting our luggage from the luggage carousel. Steven's friends were coming to meet us.

We sat and waited for our cases to appear and once we had collected them, we then went to meet Steven's friends.

They were standing at the barrier crying, then when they saw us they came forward still crying, saying "I'm so sorry!" They kept saying it over and over, by this time we were in tears too.

We walked out of the airport into the overpowering heat, it was forty seven degrees centigrade at 1:30 a.m. in the morning. I could hardly breathe.

They dropped me off at Paul's house and his dad went to stay for the first night, with Adam, Steven's best friend.

I went in, sat down in the dark. Paul's girlfriend, Grace, who had just moved out to Dubai, came down to say hi and to give me a cuddle and say she was so sorry about Steven, before going back to bed.

She was starting her new job that day. She had just gone out in the July to be with Paul, what bad timing this was for her.

I sat and waited for Paul to arrive home, his flight was getting in an hour after ours. The peace in the house was quite comforting, Steven used to live there before he had moved into an apartment just down the road.

The door opened, Paul came in, we cuddled, we cried then we went to bed, physically and mentally exhausted, we needed our rest, ready for what was to come.

Sunday 7th August

I woke at 9:00 a.m. washed and dressed and it was just as well because at 9:30 a.m. the ex knocked on my bedroom door and walked straight in, as though he had a right. He sat down and I got the usual banter from him. He was still getting at me, complaining about the holidays I had been on and saying he had no money. So nothing had changed there then.

What I was amazed at, was he knew everything about where I had been and what I had done. Yes our son had died and all that seemed to be on his mind was what I had been up to.

I told him we had to go downstairs and get on with the job in hand, we had so much to get through and we had just a week to get it all done. He said he had booked a return flight for the Thursday but I thought that there was no way we would be all done by then. I think he thought we just had to arrange to bring Steven's remains home and that was it. Unfortunately not!

I sat down at the dining table and started making lists of what we needed to do. The discussions got heated at times, if the ex thought things were not going his way, he would become very disgruntled.

We eventually received a call to say Steven's friends had found Steven's passport. Time to go to the Barsha Police Station and try and get the ball rolling. We met Steven's friend Shabs there. We needed someone who could represent us and who could speak Arabic. We just had to sit in the background feeling useless, not knowing what was being said. Paul was our spokesperson as he is an Emirates resident although he cannot speak Arabic.

We were told that they weren't releasing Steven's possessions until the next day. We couldn't see Steven, as they did not have the necessary form signed and stamped, which would allow us to go to the mortuary to see him. They explained to us that it had been a freak accident.

There was no point hanging around and so we went back to Paul's home feeling very disheartened. All I wanted was to see my boy.

When we got back to the house, Paul made several phone calls and eventually arranged for us to pick up Steven's belongings from Stefan's house, where Steven had been staying.

Ban, Steven's girlfriend came and met us there. It was the first time I had met her. I really liked her. She invited me to go and see Steven's room. I gave her a big hug and said for her to go on her own and just have some quiet time, saying goodbye to Steven. She was really grateful.

We left Stefan's and went back to Paul's house. We hadn't been in long before some of Steven's friends and their girlfriends/wives came to pay their respects. We sat and chattered, I told them stories of Steven when he was younger. The ex went outside.

I said we needed to have a memorial service, as they all needed to have closure or else they would find it very difficult to come to terms with Steven's death. I imagined they would find it really hard to cope, once we had gone back to the U.K.

Hassan, the President of the Warpigs, the Harley Davidson group Steven had been a member of, agreed to see to it and he would be in touch.

When the friends left at about 9:30 p.m. Ban took over and told us tales about Steven and his life in Dubai.

I went to bed that night and in the light of everything I was hearing, something was screaming at me that it had indeed been Steven's time to go.

It didn't make it any easier but in hindsight, on Steven's 29th birthday when I asked him what he would like to do to celebrate his 30th birthday, so that we could start planning. Steven had said to me "I don't want to be thirty, I don't want to get old!"

Four days before he passed over, Steven had posted on his Facebook page 'Looking back on my life I am surprised I am still alive.'

Did he subconsciously know? Two days before, he had shaved off his Mohican hair style, tidied his beard then on the Friday night he had met up with all of his friends and their partners to celebrate his friend Chris Topher's birthday and because he was having such a lovely night and his girlfriend hadn't been with him, Steven had rang Ban and asked if she would go and join him. She did and she said he had beamed and smiled all night.

They had slipped away, Steven on his bike and Ban in her car, travelling along behind him. She witnessed the fatal accident. It was horrendous for her but in hindsight we were able to be told about Steven a lot sooner, as Ban had rang Steven's best friend Adam, who

152

rang Paul, who rang me. Everything was as it was supposed to be.

Any questions that later came to my mind I was able to contact Ban and she would answer my questions and put my mind at rest. (She even took me to the spot where it had happened when I was in Dubai, the following April.)

These things have been so important to me, they have all helped me to cope and deal with loosing Steven and I suppose in a way move on.

That night I had phone calls from my sister and my eldest nephew. This I was truly grateful for, as they hadn't spoken to me since my mum's passing three years prior, other than on Saturday morning when I had rang my sister to tell her about Steven's death. I also received texts from my three nieces.

There is always good comes out of tragedy. I was shocked and grateful for the many messages I received via Facebook. We were being showered with love which helped to give us strength.

Monday 8th August

I must have slept for two hours at the most, I woke at 3:30 a.m. my head was full of words. I needed to write them down, so I got up, switched the light on, got my notepad and pen out and started writing. I didn't stop until 7:00 a.m.

Today, we sat around for most of the day waiting to get a phone call to say we could go back to the police station.

We actually did go back with Shabs but to no avail. Nothing had been done. So we went back to the house and started sorting through Steven's belongings. It all had to be done before we left for the U.K. I found it really hard today, his dad was in an horrendous mood and I was getting the brunt of it.

At 5:00 p.m. we eventually got the call from Shabs, to say could we meet him at the police station. Shabs had sat six hours waiting for the much needed papers to be stamped and signed. We needed these papers to enable the police to sign off some more papers which would enable us to see Steven's body.

Shabs told us he hadn't wanted us sitting waiting for them, so he had gone himself, God bless him. We met him at the police station, he was wearing a black T shirt bearing the words 'Steve hope you are in a better place' with a print of Steven's face on the back of it. It touched my heart.

We went inside and upstairs to the traffic division. At first the policeman told us that they were about to close for the day but Shabs explained that we had travelled to Dubai on Saturday from the U.K. and as yet we still hadn't been allowed to see our deceased son.

The policeman looked at his watch, thought for a moment then saw to the much needed papers. Brilliant, we could go and see Steven. We drove to the other side of Dubai, to the mortuary only to find it closed. My heart sank, I still hadn't got to see my boy and we

154

would have to wait another day. Our hopes had been dashed and we were all very subdued on the way home.

My sister rang on the evening and I asked her if she could contact the undertaker and ask him if he could do Steven's funeral. She rang straight back, yes there would be no problem, everything was in place, one less thing to worry about.

The undertaker actually rang me and told me not to worry they would indeed take care of Steven. So the wheels had been put in motion, so to speak.

I sat for a while but I could feel the atmosphere getting worse by the minute, so I took myself off and had a much welcome soak in the bath. I needed to be in a toxic atmosphere, like a hole in the head.

The ex, when we were sorting out Steven's possessions, had been saying he needed them, without any consideration as to whether or not I might like some keepsakes too. I got really upset in my bedroom and said to Paul, when he came up to see if I was okay, that I was Steven's mum, I too would like some of Steven's possessions as keepsakes. Not that I needed anything to remember him by, his memory is engrained in my heart.

Paul went away and brought Steven's Mont Blanc keyring and pen. He gave me a big hug and said everything would be okay. I had earlier found Steven's watch in my bedside drawer and had given it to Paul, it was just right that Paul should have his brother's watch.

Steven always loved a good pen, watch and sunglasses (shades) otherwise he wasn't materialistic, well saying that he loved his technology, everything Apple. I had just bought both my boys an Apple watch the previous Christmas, something had told me to get them and I am so pleased I had. Steven had been ecstatic when he had opened his present.

I will treasure his pen, as I love to write and his keyring, well it immediately went onto my keyring.

Tuesday 9th August

Well today's the day! We were up very early and out at the crack of dawn, not stopping to have breakfast. We had arranged to meet Shabs at the mortuary. We arrived there and had to wait quite a while before the mortician came and got us.

He opened the door and we followed behind him, a gentleman dressed in green theatre gear came towards us, wheeling a trolley with Steven's body on it, which was encased in a body bag and above his head was a huge tuft, where they had gathered and tied all of the material. It was grotesque and not how I expected to see my son.

(It took me a long time over the days, weeks, months that followed, to get rid of this image in my head.)

We were standing in the middle of the corridor and this gentleman was saying, "Be quick, hurry, hurry, it is so hot."

I looked at my boy lying there so still, only his face was visible. I was aware of where they had carried out the post mortem, his left shoulder was so deformed, it was up against his ear and his beard had grown long and curly.

We each had a few moments with him, we didn't know if that would be the last time we would see him. It was so hard, I wanted to stay with him, no way did I want to leave. But by the time we were shown out, I felt a lot easier.

Next stop, the British Embassy to get Steven's passport cancelled. This was another ordeal. It was like getting into Fort Knox, we had to leave our mobile phones at the Reception desk. We were taken to another room where they scanned us with a detector before we were allowed to go through another door which lead us to the outside quadrangle, which was surrounded by high fencing.

It was like being in a prison. We walked along a pathway then came to another building and after going through two more doors, we came to a line of people sitting behind a screen, it reminded me of when you walk into a bank.

We went up to one of the desks, gave the name of who we needed to see then had to sit down and wait. After a few minutes this person came and took us along a corridor to a room, where there was an older gentleman who was visiting from England, sitting there.

He asked if we minded him being in on the meeting but also explained that he had just lost his sister at Easter in a car crash. He was very sympathetic towards us.

We sat down, answered a few questions then the lady cancelled Steven's passport, stamped the necessary forms by which time we were allowed to go. I have to say they didn't do a lot but at the same time they were really pleasant towards us.

We actually managed to stop and have some lunch today, eating has not been a priority these past couple of days, I still had the lump in my throat and had no appetite.

Afterwards we went to pick up Steven's possessions which had been stored at Hassan's house.

When Steven had been made redundant in May 2016, he had met up with his friends and when he had informed them of his redundancy, they had sent Steven off to the toilet, asking him to give them ten minutes. Whilst he was gone they had quickly had a meeting and decided that if Steven gave up his apartment, they would each take it in turn, to have Steven stay with them until such a time when he had his business up and running.

The business he had dreamed of owning, Hustle Cycles. They also clubbed together and gave Steven living expenses each week, enabling Steven to have no worries. It had all been sorted in about ten minutes at a meeting of the Warpigs. Their generosity towards him had been outstanding.

Steven was planning to build custom Harley Davidsons, besides servicing motor bikes and doing welding jobs. He had already built his own 'Black Betty.'

Steven had also given Paul his personal possessions for safe keeping when he gave up his apartment. In hindsight again it was as if he was making things easy for us.

It had taken us a while to find Hassan's house, as we were not used to this area of Dubai and fortunately he had refreshments waiting for us when we arrived. It was fifty two degrees outside. My lungs felt as if they were burning. I had never experienced anything like this in my life, in more ways than one.

Paul and his dad loaded everything onto the back of the truck, Ban was also with us and had been all day. Rather than leave her to travel on her own, I had been riding with her, in her car. It was really quite special because as she drove, she talked about Steven, things I might never have otherwise known.

When they were all done, we headed back to Paul's, where after we had had dinner, we started sorting out all of the boxes.

You might think we should have waited to do this, it was so soon after Steven had passed but there was no time to be sentimental, we just had to get on with the jobs in hand. Time was against us and no way did I want to leave these jobs for Paul to do, after we had returned to the U.K., after all he was only twenty one.

We sorted out all of Steven's clothes, all of his Warpig items went back to the club. His guitar we gave to Dave, his friend who he used to 'strum' with on a night. The rest of Steven's clothing we packed up ready to take to a Christian church. At least they could distribute them to the needy and hopefully help others. Finally his pride possession, his Black Betty, the bike he had custom built, we gave to the The Warpigs Club.

We were right in the midst of things when Danielle, Steven's really good and close friend, who Steven had called his Chunky Monkey, even though she is beautiful and slim, arrived to see us, she was so upset.

I will never forget her text last Saturday morning saying she had just seen a posting on Facebook saying that Steven had died and to please tell her that it wasn't true. It was heartbreaking. Steven had actually got Danielle a job in Dubai, shortly after he had arrived there himself.

I gave her a couple of his T-shirts so that when she needed to, she could wear one for bed and feel him close to her. She stayed until about 10:00 p.m. then said bye and I went off to bed.

I sat in bed for quite some time, looking at the photos I had of Steven on my phone and also listening to some music. 5:00 a.m. sleep just would not come. I think I eventually must have nodded off and maybe I had a couple of hours sleep in total.

Wednesday 10th August

We set out to go to the police station at 10:10 a.m. I had become aware that I was receiving Divine guidance from God. I found I was knowing facts without knowing how I received the information.

Today we got our last document stamped. We all heaved a huge sigh of relief. Once this was done our task today was to go in search of a Christian Church, enabling us to donate Steven's clothes to the church so that they could distribute them to the needy. We found it, actually we found a row of churches in the middle of nowhere, the Christian one being the last in the row.

I went in search of someone, all of the church doors were open but not a soul was in sight. Paul and his dad unloaded the bags and stacked them at the back of the church, whilst I went in search of a piece of paper to write a message on it, so that they would know where they had come from.

Once everything was stacked, I placed the note on the top of the bags and boxes, Paul and his dad went back to the truck and I went and sat in a pew and prayed. I was just about finished when I heard voices coming from outside the door at the back of the church. I went outside and found a black lady making her way into the lift, at the side of the church. She stopped when she saw me.

I explained why and what I was doing there. She looked at the watch on her wrist and then informed me that the priest was due in about five minutes, would I like to wait and I said yes I would. So she took me up in the lift with her to the offices, she gave me a bottle of water and asked me to sit down.

I must have just been there a few minutes when the priest walked in.

He was Greek/Cypriot and as soon as I explained my reason for being there, his eyes filled up with unshed tears. He had three daughters aged 24, 26 and 30 of his own and said he could not even envisage the pain I must be going through. He took me down the corridor to a room on the right. We went inside, sat down and he said prayers. I was so grateful. Afterwards I went back to the truck with a lighter heart and feeling so much calmer and more peaceful.

I had wanted a church memorial service here in Dubai but that wasn't to be. I had given my request up to God and remarkably my wish had been granted but not in the way I had thought. I had had prayers in a Christian church and we were having a memorial gathering in a hotel the following evening after we had attended a memorial ride with the Warpigs, which was in Steven's memory.

I have learnt over the years that if we give our problems up to God, He can sort them out so much better than we ever can, plus without having to worry about them.

A quick stop off at McDonalds for a late lunch on the go, as our next stop was finding the place where we had to change the log book and registration of Steven's car, into Paul's name, so that Paul could drive it.

Almost finished for the day, we only had to go to Stefan's house to pick up Steven's car and take it back to Paul's house. Paul and his dad decided to take it through a car wash, as it looked as though it had been through a sandstorm, which I suppose was quite possible.

Whilst Paul and his dad did that, I took the opportunity to have a cool shower back at Paul's house, the temperature today was only thirty nine degrees but it still felt unbearable.

After tea we received a message from another one of Steven's friends, Chris, who was wanting us to WhatsApp some of our photos to him, that we had of Steven on our phones. He was preparing something for the memorial gathering which the Warpigs were organising for the following evening.

As we sat discussing the funeral, I happened to say that I was sure there was a Harley Davidson hearse back in England. His dad googled it and indeed there was. We could not believe our luck as it was based in Sunderland, where we were going to hold Steven's funeral.

Ban came over to Paul's that night and we all sat and talked and tried to select which music we would have played at Steven's funeral back in the U.K.

I couldn't believe it, the 'ex' actually agreed with me that we should have this song which had played every time we had been out in the truck, when we were out and about on our travels. The song was Spirits by the Rumbalas.

When I first heard it, I couldn't believe my ears, I asked Paul to turn the radio up and do what he does on his phone, to find out what the song was and who sang it.

I listened to the words and they were telling me;

"Guns in my head and they won't go." Steven had had a brain haemorrhage.

"Spirits in my head and they won't go." They were coming to take him home.

"He didn't want to live forever, but he wanted to be alive!" Steven hadn't been ready to go, he was happy, his life was great, his business had taken off and he had his soulmate at his side.

This song played on the radio every day, until his dad agreed that we should include it with the other songs we had chosen to have played at Steven's funeral. After that we didn't hear the song again. Steven was letting me know in no uncertain terms exactly what had happened.

Ban left and we all agreed we needed an early night, we had a very early start again in the morning.

A year later I had just had a tattoo done of Steven's name in Arabic on my wrist, Steven's friend Jane had taken me to have it done. Afterwards, as we were having lunch in a restaurant, in the background we heard the Rumbala's song being played. I am sure it was Steven giving me confirmation that he loved the tattoo. It was the one thing I could have had done which he would have so approved of.

Thursday 11th August

My phone pinged at 3:00 a.m. and that was it, as far as sleep goes. I wrote to my friend Jan in America, letting her know how things were going and I read and finished off the words that I had written two days before, which was to be Steven's eulogy. By which time it was time to start a new day.

We were all up and out of the house by 7 a.m. on our way to meet Shabs at the mortuary. When we arrived, we had to sit in the waiting room, until someone came to get us.

Suddenly this security man pointed at me and made signs that I had to go and sit behind the screen with the women.

This really shook me, I was in such a state at the fact I was being segregated. I sat down behind the screen and I started to cry, I just couldn't help myself, it felt awful.

Paul came and got me, he said "Come on mam, come and stand beside me." Which I did but it had knocked my confidence and it was taking every bit of strength to prepare myself for what was to come. I didn't know what was expected of us.

After a while they came and got us and took us to a reception desk at the back of the mortuary, where we waited for Steven's body to be wheeled out again on a trolley. We had to sign to say it was indeed Steven's remains and then watch as they transferred his body into the back of an ambulance ready to take him to the embalmer.

We stood and watched, hardly comprehending what we were witnessing. As the ambulance drove away we realised that no-one had even offered to give us Steven's personal possessions.

We were expected to follow the ambulance but I said "Where are Steven's possessions? We have received nothing."

The guard went away and brought out a small plastic bag which contained Steven's wallet and his two Warpigs rings. So I asked again "But where are all of his other things?"

Again the guard went away and this time he brought out another small plastic bag but this time it held two condoms. Well if nothing else, it broke the atmosphere.

I laughed and said "That's my boy, staying safe, God bless him."

The look on the guards faces was like thunder. They don't approve of sex before marriage!

Well I had to ask again and this time he brought out a large blue plastic bag containing Steven's clothes. Shabs went to take them but I said that I wanted them, I would give him them back but I just needed them for a short while.

We went outside into the blazing heat, got into our cars and we followed Shabs to the embalmer. As we travelled along, Paul driving with his dad sitting beside him in the front, I was sitting in the back of the truck, I opened the blue plastic bag and took each item out, one by one.

My first reaction was why only one shoe and no socks, Steven always wore those trainer socks. His bikers' Warpigs leather waistcoat was stiff and stained with blood. I laid it on my knee and closed my eyes. In my mind I could feel and see him laying his head on my knees and I was stroking his soft silky hair, for just one last time.

I sat like that for a few moments, in my own world saying goodbye to my darling boy. I opened my eyes and put everything back inside the blue plastic bag and when we got to our destination, the embalmers, I handed the blue bag over to Shabs.

We were really seeing the other side of Dubai, as the embalmers was situated next to the workhouses. The people who live here are Indian people. They do all the hard graft in Dubai, building work, work on the roads, everything to do with maintenance. This was where they lived, sharing rooms. One person who worked on days would sleep in the bed at night and then the person working on nights would sleep in the bed during the day.

It's sad to see but these people are so grateful, it means they can afford to send money back to their families, enabling them to have a better quality of life back in India.

Once we had gotten over the shock of seeing these poor people, we went inside the embalmers and were asked to wait. They told us that there was a form missing and so Shabs went back to the mortuary to retrieve it.

In the meantime we sat in a very basic, very bottle green room, yes everything in this building was bottle green, the walls and the floors. There was very little furniture, in fact if I remember correctly there were only two chairs for visitors, a desk and the guy who was obviously the receptionist. Paul had to stand beside us.

We waited here until they had embalmed Steven's body and prepared him for his final journey. Once they had done what they needed to do and we had paid them, we were shown into what I could only describe as an empty ward. The only thing in it were curtains hanging, sectioning off the different cubicles but they were all drawn back, so it was a very stark green room with Steven's body, in a coffin, on a trolley, in the middle of it.

Steven looked so much better, he was out of the body bag, thank goodness and they had straightened his shoulder and trimmed and combed his beard, he looked so much more like my boy.

So much so, that I asked his dad to go and get Paul. Paul had said he didn't need to see Steven again but I told his dad to tell him that Steven looked so much better and I thought he needed to see him as he was.

His dad went and got Paul and they came back. Paul was so pleased we had done so, as he felt better for seeing Steven so much more comfortable and looking more like Steven.

This was the last time we would see Steven before his journey back to the U.K. inside the lead lined coffin.

Why lead lined you might ask? Well it is to stop any infection leaking out of the coffin. Apparently, so I was told, the air con on an aeroplane is circulated throughout the plane even in the hold and so if there was any infection and it leaked out, then it would be circulated into the cabin causing infection to spread. You learn something every day.

We said our goodbyes to him, then they wheeled the coffin away, to seal it and prepare for it to be taken to the Emirates Cargo Depot, where we had to go next, to book the coffin on to our flight.

We walked back into reception just as Shabs arrived back with the missing document. We told Shabs that we had just seen Steven and how much better he had looked. Shabs excused himself and ran off to see if he too could see Steven but they were just putting the last nail into his coffin, literally.

He returned to where we were waiting, saddened by the fact that he had missed his chance of saying goodbye. We said goodbye to Shabs, who apologised but he would have to leave us now as he was in great need of a visit to the hospital. He was suffering with tonsillitis and had suffered in silence whilst he had helped us do all of the necessities which we had had to do. He had put our needs before his own. He had been our translator, as everywhere we went they had only spoken Arabic. He had been really marvellous, we were so grateful to him, we will be forever in his debt.

We had no time to ponder or grieve, well I suppose we had our moments when one of us would loose it big time. We literally had until Thursday at 5:30 p.m. to get everything done because official buildings are not open on a Friday in Dubai and we were booked to fly home on the Saturday.

So we were on our way now to the Emirates Cargo Department to sort out all the legalities and paperwork to allow us to book Steven's coffin into cargo. It took quite a while and Hassan, Steven's close friend, who works there, came to see us, to make sure all was going well. He told us everything had been arranged for that evening for a memorial ride in Steven's memory and then we would meet up afterwards at an hotel where we would have a memorial gathering.

We thanked him for organising it and said how much we appreciated everything everyone had done for us. Paul completed the booking, may I say Paul because he is an Emirates resident had to deal with all of the authorities. His dad and I just had to sit and be there for moral support. I was so proud of him, being twenty one and dealing with all that he had had to do, he was amazing but also I felt for him, as he had had very little time to grieve his big brother's passing.

We heaved a sigh of relief as we left the building, we had managed to get it all done within the week because if we had not, we would have had to change our flights back to the U.K. Well his dad did have to, as he had been booked to fly back to the U.K. today.

Okay, so we took a breather, Paul had to go for petrol and as he did so, he purchased a bag of crisps, a chocolate bar and a drink for each of us, yes that was breakfast and lunch combined but we had a busy afternoon, no time to stop to eat.

Our next job was to go to the courts, we had to get Power of Attorney for Paul to carry out anything that

170

might crop up after we had returned home. It took three courts in all. But first we had to get on the phone and arrange for one of Paul's friends and another of Steven's friends, Dave, to meet us, we needed two witnesses. We also had to find the courts, which were all in different places and time was against us.

The minutes, hours were ticking away and panic was setting in, especially the last court which wouldn't allow Paul in because he was wearing shorts. I sent him off to buy a pair of trousers, any, just as long as his legs were covered but he must be quick, as time was not on our side.

Well we all laughed when we saw him come back, in a pair of very baggy tracksuit bottoms which were too long for him. Paul may I add is a very stylish young man, who would normally not be seen dead in baggy tracksuit bottoms, so he was way out of his comfort zone, but it did lighten the mood.

We were standing in the queue, waiting to be attended to, we had already been interviewed and told what forms were required once our number was called by the typing pool. We then had to sit and wait for the documents to be typed, before queueing to pay for the typing of them.

We had to laugh again, as when Paul came to pay for the documents, he was standing, without looking at what he was doing, trying to put his hand in his pocket, forgetting he had the trousers on top of his shorts. It was like something from You've Been Framed. These little things certainly helped to ease the tension of the job in hand.

Panic was rising, as we stood in the queue waiting to be seen to by a member in the court. I have never known time tick by so quickly, too quickly for our liking. We were just beginning to think we would not be seen in time, when a gentleman from room No.13 came out and waved us over.

Steven's lucky number was 13, he had it tattooed on his bottom, it was the first tattoo he had ever had. Our boy was looking after us.

The guy was joking and carrying on with us and when he asked why Paul and not his mum needed the Power of Attorney, the gentleman was mortified when we told him the reason why. He was so apologetic for joking and carrying on, that he came out with us and made sure we got priority in the queue to pay for this service.

We eventually got out of the courts at 5 p.m. We were meeting the bikers between 6:00-6:30 p.m. at the garage opposite the Harley Davidson dealership, on Sheikh Zayed Road where we were going to follow behind them in Paul's truck, on the memorial ride.

There was no messing about, we quickly said goodbye and thanked the two guys who had been witnesses for us before we got into the truck and quickly made our way home. We arrived back at Paul's at 5:30 p.m. we each had to be showered, changed and ready to go by 6 p.m. We didn't have a minute leeway. We made it by the skin of our teeth.

The forty bikes were all lined up, we were introduced to each and every one of the bikers and then it was time to leave. Paul and I got inside the truck, his dad stood in

172

front of the bikers and took a video of them as they slowly got into line and rode off. It was both exhilarating and amazing, Steven would have been so chuffed that his mum had participated on a 'ride', be it in a truck.

Steven had once, back in the U.K. taken me for a spin on the back of his Harley Davidson, one night after work. Happy memories, very happy ones.

Whilst Paul and I were sitting waiting to move off in the truck, a biker wearing white shades came towards us, (no biker wears white shades) I looked and said "Dear God it's Steven!" To which Paul replied "Jesus Christ!" We never saw that biker again. I truly believe Steven was letting us know he was okay and riding high.

The noise of the Warpigs and Black Eagles bikes (two Harley Davidson clubs Steven used to ride with) roaring off into the distance was phenomenal, the adrenaline in our blood was pumping like nothing I had ever experienced.

Paul slowly moved off, stopped to pick his dad up on the way, then we just stayed at the back of the pack. We rode for half an hour before coming to the Grand Excelsior Hotel. The bikers were already parked up and starting to go inside. We followed, obviously not knowing where to go.

We were taken upstairs to a room which was filled with people. I was truly amazed, there was more than eighty people in the room. Steven had well and truly found his true family.

Just inside the door was a Book of Remembrance, custom made by the guys, with Steven's photo on the front, with nuts and bolts screwed in to the cover and a chain, like what he wore on the side of his jeans, on the side of the book.

Cards with a photo of Steven standing by his custom made bike, his Black Betty, printed on it and words of a Heavy Metal song, which was apparently too heavy to be played on the night, waiting for people to take one, as a keepsake of the evening.

The room was divided into two semi circles and at the front there was a screen and a lectern and at the back stood an easel with a large print resting on it, of Steven smiling. Beside the easel, on a pedestal, stood a vase of the most exquisite white roses I have ever seen. Steven would have been so shocked and amazed that this was all in his memory.

Everyone sat down and prompt 7:30 p.m. the proceedings started with Hassan, the Warpigs President, welcoming everyone and then he handed over to me. I stood up, went to the lectern and said a few prayers before reading the eulogy, which I had written earlier in the week. You could hear a pin drop. Paul was next to speak, telling everyone just what his big brother had meant to him. His dad stood and thanked everyone for coming then one by one his closest friends stood up and said what Steven had meant to them.

To finish the formal part of the evening, Chris showed us a presentation which he had prepared, of Steven's life. It was fantastic, the one thing that came across to everyone was that Steven had been the happiest he had ever been in his short life, here in Dubai. He grinned like a Cheshire cat on most of the photographs. He had indeed found his niche in life and a wonderful set of friends to go with it. The number of people present in that room was a credit to him. He would never have said that he was so popular nor that people thought so much of him. For me, his mum, it was a true comfort.

The official part of the evening was over, the bikers had put refreshments on for everyone and people started to mingle. I had lots of people coming up and introducing themselves to me and telling me what Steven had meant to them. My boy had been well and truly loved and accepted, tattoos and all.

I suddenly noticed Hassan sitting breaking his heart. I went over and comforted him. He was taking Steven's death very badly, he could not believe that his most loyal friend was no more. If I am truly honest, everyone else was finding it hard to. It had been a huge shock which no-one had expected nor wanted.

About 10:00 p.m. most people had by then, slowly drifted off, whether to go and have a drink in the bar or to go home.

We picked up all of the items and headed for home but not before we had a stop off at McDonalds for something to eat. I would not normally touch McDonalds with a barge pole but this week I have been very grateful for their food. Because we had been talking to people all evening, we still had not had time to eat.

We arrived home at 10:45 p.m. takeaways in hand and sat down with some of Paul's friends and Ban and we reflected upon the evening.

If I am honest, we didn't want the evening to end, we were all on a high. It had been so lovely and there had been so much love for Steven in that room, I wished I could have bottled it up and brought some of it back to the U.K.

What a fitting and most beautiful tribute in memory of our beautiful son and brother. Thank you Lord, it meant so much to us.

One thing for sure was he had had some very special people in his life and I could see why he had always said that he would never come back to the U.K.

Dubai certainly does have some sort of magic about it, it is a beautiful place full of beautiful, happy, people. It certainly has bewitched me.

The euphoria of the evening sort of lifted all of us after the traumatic week we had had and in a way sort of recharged our batteries ready for the next part of Steven's journey.

And so at 2:15 a.m. we all eventually went to bed, the end of another chapter. We just had Steven's final journey and his funeral to his place of rest to get through.

Friday 12th August

We had a lie in this morning, we weren't leaving until 10 a.m. so a little bit later than our 7 a.m.'s of late. Our final day in Dubai and the first thing we had to do was to go back to Emirates Cargo to pay for the transit of Steven's coffin back to the U.K. and to check that it would definitely be on our flight.

All done, we met with Ban at the Irish Village for a late brunch and to say our farewells. I worried, when we left her, as to whether she would be able to cope once we were back in the U.K. She was only twenty five and what she had endured this past week was what most people would never have to do, in a lifetime.

The only other thing we needed to do today was, we had to go to Paul's boss's home and exchange trucks and to see Paul's friend Danny who had just arrived that day with his girlfriend. They were staying there because they should have been staying with Paul but due to circumstances, we were instead.

We got back to Paul's house early afternoon, I started to feel panicky, I didn't want to leave Dubai, I felt Steven's spirit was there in Dubai, plus I didn't want to leave Paul there on his own after all he had been through.

Paul was following on later, as he had work to do, plus we didn't know how long it would take before we could have Steven's funeral. I suppose there was also the reality of once back in the U.K. we had to start again organising the funeral.

We decided that because Grace's parents had arrived in Dubai the previous day for a planned holiday, we should really meet up with them and go for a meal. If I was honest, I was not hungry, it was like chewing cardboard. I truly struggled with the meal but afterwards I sat and chattered with Lesley, Grace's mum, reflecting on the past week. The highs and lows and the absolutely horrendous, not knowing how we had gotten through it but we had survived what can only be described as a tsunami in our lives.

We had been told it would take us three weeks to get everything sorted in Dubai and we had managed with a lot of help from Steven's friends to complete everything in just six days. We are eternally grateful to all of Steven's friends for their constant love, help and support.

We weren't long in saying farewell to Graham and Lesley, we had to pack and be up at 4:30 a.m. in the morning, to get our 7:40 a.m. flight back to Newcastle.

I really wasn't feeling very good when we got back to Paul's, I became very tearful, misplacing things, so much so, I had to shout for Paul to see if he could come and help me. 12:08 a.m. I eventually lay down and put my head on the pillow, not that it was going to be there for long.

Saturday 13th August

Paul dropped us off at the airport and it was a very tearful goodbye, I really didn't want to leave him. His dad and I got booked in, had something to eat and tried to relax as we waited for our flight. We boarded, this time we were both travelling Economy, I was sat in front of him. Flying home today, would I ever have thought that I would be flying on a plane with my son's remains in the hold. I was really not looking forward to this journey.

I had nodded off to sleep, I am sure it was before we had even left the runway. I was both physically and mentally exhausted.

About an hour into the flight, the steward came and took both of us into Business Class. I was so grateful, at least we could get some rest.

My friend Margaret was waiting to take me home, as we came through Customs at Newcastle Airport. She had brought some food with her to make us some lunch once we arrived back at my house. We sat and talked, I told her all that had happened over the past week. She left about 3:00 p.m. as she could see how exhausted I was, it all felt like a nightmare now that I was back home in the U.K.

I received a phone call shortly after she left, from the undertakers, to say Steven was now safely in their care and residing in their Chapel of Rest.

There was a pile of bereavement cards waiting for me, I made a cup of coffee, sat down and slowly opened and read them, the tears dripping off my chin. I had to keep stopping, wipe my eyes, try and take a deep breath but yes it wasn't just a horrible nightmare, my precious, darling boy was no more.

The reality was kicking in, I had had so much to do and so many young ones needing a strong mother figure to tell them it was all going to be okay, that I had, I guess, put my feelings, for the majority of the time, locked away but now I was home, they were all gushing back, now I was on my own, in my own home.

I had a continuous flow of visitors who sat and kept me company until it was time for bed, I had been up almost twenty two hours. I was so grateful I had had company as I didn't feel like being on my own, but now I was exhausted.

Sunday 14th August

Even though I had been so tired, I still woke early. I sat and listened to Steven's music and watched Chris's presentation again. He had given us each a copy to bring home.

By 7:30 a.m. I was showered, dressed and ready to go to 8 a.m. service at church. When I got there, I sat quietly praying, when suddenly the sun shone through the window above the altar. I thought that's it, that's the hymn we should have for Steven's funeral, 'I Watch The Sunrise!' Steven loved to be out in the desert and to watch the sunrise.

Afterwards the priest chattered to me, saying he was sorry about Steven's death and he asked how we had got on the previous week. I told him about the tribute ride the bikers had done in Steven's memory and how we had managed to locate a Harley hearse in Sunderland where it just so happened was where we were having his funeral. I told him how I would have loved to have a bikers' escort behind the hearse. The reason being, Steven had ridden with the Harley riders in Tyneside on a Wednesday evening when he worked at the Harley Davidson dealership at Silverlink.

The priest said he used to be a biker and his friend rode a Harley, would I like him to give his friend my details to enable him to contact me. I agreed wholeheartedly and said that would be fantastic, I would really appreciate it.

I had a continuous flow of visitors all day, not counting the number of phone calls and text messages. By bedtime I was again exhausted, but it helped me to go to sleep.

Monday 15th August

I woke today feeling exhausted, I think everything was taking it's toll on me. I got up, showered and dressed then went for a walk. As I walked, I talked to God asking for strength to get through the hours, days, weeks, months, years ahead of me, without my son.

Afterwards, I felt calm and comforted.

I had visitors all day, one couple who came, were our old neighbours, Kath and Dave. They had been our neighbours when Steven had been born and had been quite a part of his life as he was growing up. They hadn't known of Steven's death, they had just been out for a ride and something had told them to call in. They had not even been to my new house, they had just called on the off chance. You can imagine what a shock they got.

I was so grateful to everyone, they were giving me strength to carry on but I was so exhausted.

Tuesday 16th August

A new day dawns but before it even starts I know it is going to be a hard one to get through. 8:15 a.m. I was in my car heading towards Sunderland. I had to go to the boys' dad's house first before we both had to go to the undertakers, where we had an appointment with the assistant coroner.

We had to meet the assistant coroner there to enable us to verify that it was indeed Steven's remains in the coffin, which the undertakers had collected from the airport on the Saturday afternoon.

There were more forms to sign, once the assistant coroner was satisfied that everything that he needed to do, was done. He took his leave saying the coroner could possibly request another post mortem and it could take a week before we could possibly get the okay to go ahead and plan Steven's funeral.

After he left we then had to start the proceedings with the undertaker.

The first thing the undertaker asked us was what type of coffin did we want? I couldn't understand this, as

Steven was already in a coffin but he went on to explain that unfortunately the coffin was stamped with cargo all over it.

"But it was my son's body, not cargo!!!" I said.

This deeply upset me.

There were moments during this meeting, which became tense, when the 'ex' and I couldn't agree. We now didn't have Paul to have his say and to calm the storm and be mediator. We did however get through it.

Apparently we were told some divorced couples this happens to, just cannot agree, so I suppose we were getting somewhere.

All done, we had to make our way back to the ex's house to meet the priest. We talked through the service, the 'ex' had left this to me, as I am the one who goes to church on a regular basis or at least I used to, I suppose I was more knowledgeable about what was required.

The priest wanted to know which hymn to play as Steven's coffin was being carried in to church. I said we didn't want a hymn, we would like Steven's music played as people were arriving. I explained that my friend, Marian was making us a C.D. of all the music we wanted playing and we would get it to him before the service.

Stairway to Heaven by Led Zeppelin, we wanted played as the coffin was being carried in to church.

To come out of church, Knocking on Heaven's Door by Guns n'Roses.

The other songs were:-

Sweet Child of Mine by Guns n'Roses,

Sound of Silence by Disturbed,

Spirits by The Rumbalas,

God's Gonna Cut You Down by Johnny Cash.

All to be played whilst people were arriving for the service.

We had already chosen the hymn 'I Watch The Sunrise' but we needed a second hymn and I asked if we could have the 23rd Psalm, I had noticed that one of Steven's friends had posted it on Facebook that very day. The ex said it was quite appropriate because the bikers wore the Number 23 on the back of their leather waistcoats under the Warpigs name. I said that was it, that was the confirmation we needed and so we had the 23rd Psalm.

Just then I received a phone call from the coroner's assistant to say that there was no need for a further post mortem as the cause of death was conclusive. He was indeed giving us the go ahead to plan the funeral. The one week had become three hours.

Everything was working in our favour and fate was on our side.

We showed the priest Chris's presentation which he had done for us in Dubai and he told us that we needed to show this to everyone, as Steven looked so happy. I said I thought that when you had a church service you only were able to have prayers at the crematorium. He said normally that was the case but what he would do would be to say the prayers then go out and the undertaker would show the presentation whilst everyone sat and watched.

I was thrilled, he was so amenable and helpful, Steven would have loved that. And so it was, the funeral service after a two hour discussion and presentation was complete. We said farewell to the priest and we ourselves had to leave.

The priest rang us back within the hour to say there was a slot at the crematorium for the following Monday and he was available that day, so the date was set, Monday 22nd August 2016.

Next job, ordering the flowers and the family had asked if we would order their flowers too. We decided the ex, Paul and I would have a wreath in the shape of a Harley Davidson, and his aunties, uncles and cousins would have two wreaths between them all, one a Flying V Guitar and the other a Hand of Cards, representing his love of biking, music and magic. His three great loves.

The only thing left to organise was the venue for afterwards, we couldn't have it in the church hall because that was fully booked. We went to the local pub but the manager couldn't even be bothered to come downstairs to see us and so we went to another pub which was about a mile along the road. They couldn't have been more helpful, even though the manager was away on his holidays, yes they would do everything they could to make sure everything ran smoothly. What a difference!

We decided to sit down and have something to eat, as it was now teatime. It had been a long, emotional, tiring day but we had got everything we needed to do, done. I couldn't believe that as we were eating, the ex started to bring up the past, as if I didn't have enough to deal with. He just couldn't let go.

We went back to his home and started to sort out the things he had of Steven's. By 6 p.m. I was both exhausted and drained. We were done, I left and instead of driving the twenty six miles home, I called at my old neighbour's, Maria, asking if she wouldn't mind making me a cuppa before I made the journey home, I didn't trust myself driving, I was so tired.

Maria made me a sandwich and a coffee and we sat and talked over what had happened that day.

I didn't stay too long as I had one more call to make to my friends, Gill and Roy, who were going to take Steven's old Ice Hockey gear to Whitley Bay Ice Rink, where Steven used to play for the Whitley Bay Warriors. Their daughter lived nearby and they said they didn't mind dropping the items off. I just wanted someone to have the use of his things, maybe there was someone who wanted to play but couldn't afford to buy the equipment needed.

Gill and Roy wouldn't let me drive home, they could see how exhausted I was. Instead they offered me a bed for the night. I was truly grateful as I said earlier, I was so exhausted.

The priest had requested that I send him a copy of the eulogy I had written and what I was going to read out on the day of the funeral but something made me, when I sent it, miss off the last paragraph. I would just read it out on the day.

When I had written the eulogy in Dubai, I had ended by saying "That our children are a gift from God and when He needs them to go back, we have to give them willingly, as His needs are greater than ours."

In Dubai when I read it, a few mothers had come up to me and commented on this. They thought they owned their children, when in fact they are just on loan to us.

(It happened again the day of the funeral and I have to say as I was writing this, I was prompted to put it in again.)

The ex also demanded I omit certain things I had said in the eulogy in Dubai and if I did not then he would have to stand up and say something, (more controlling.)

I thought it wasn't about him, the eulogy was about Steven but my ego wasn't in need and maybe his was and so I did what he demanded and thought it doesn't matter. What I said in Dubai, had to be said in Dubai, which I had done. Mission accomplished.

Wednesday 17th August

I woke at 3:00 a.m. with 'A Sound of Silence' playing in my head. It's constantly there. I put the light on, put my specs on and started to make a list of everything I needed to do but it was all at home today, thank goodness.

I got up as soon as I could, had an early breakfast, said bye to Gill and Roy and thanked them for their hospitality then set off. But before I left Sunderland, I called to have just a quick coffee with my friend

Margaret, the one who had come to be with me when Steven died. I just felt she needed an update and it was also courtesy, as I was in the area. Coffee drunk, a quick hug, then I was homeward bound.

Once I was home, showered and changed, I felt quite human again.

Fortunately I had no visitors until 7:00 p.m., just lots of phone calls. I received three bouquets and ninety bereavement cards. Everyone was being so kind and I think Steven's death had been such a shock to everyone.

It was 11:30 p.m. before the last visitor left, I so appreciated everyone taking time out of their lives to be with me, as I was finding it really quite hard to cope, especially being on my own.

Thursday 18th August

It was another very early start today as I had to leave home at 7:30 a.m. to go straight to the undertakers.

Steven's remains were deteriorating fast and I just wanted to see him for one last time and place a red rose in the coffin alongside photos of his girlfriend, friends, Paul, his dad and myself with messages on the back of each one of them.

I also placed his 'Peng' a little penguin he had had since birth which he loved and had even took to Dubai with him, a packet of cigarettes, he never went anywhere without his cigs and last but not least a pack of cards, as again, he always had a pack of cards with him. He would do card tricks in a bar, work, anywhere really. They all went with him in the coffin.

When I arrived, my eldest niece Judith and her daughter Megan were already there waiting for me. I went in first, I wasn't sure what to expect as they said they had had to do some repairs that morning. I could see straight away that the skin on Steven's nose was becoming very thin and I could see where they had patched it up. It was quite upsetting but I suppose that it was now twelve days since Steven had passed over.

Put all that to one side, Steven looked the best I had seen him in these past twelve days, he actually looked at rest. I also noted that his hand had turned black and after we said our last farewells to him, I asked the undertaker to seal the coffin, his dad and his Aunty Joy and cousins had been the day before. I wanted no-one else to see the deterioration.

I had a coffee at my niece's house then left to go back home. I think travelling a fifty two mile round trip, was taking it's toll plus the emotions and everything else you go through at this time. I felt truly exhausted, my body felt as though it was giving up on me. I was struggling to keep going. It felt like I was in a bubble watching people on the outside getting on with their lives whilst mine had just been blown to pieces.

On the journey home, I struggled to keep awake, I honestly felt as if I was going to go to sleep at the wheel. I was so relieved when I eventually pulled up at my house. I gave thanks to God for getting me home safely.

I went in, sat down in my chair by the fire and slept, I can't remember how long but I slept for England.

Everything had caught up with me, my body told me it needed to rest, it couldn't go on.

I don't think I did anything for the rest of the day. The biker Paul, who was a friend of my local priest, rang me on the evening to ask for my permission to put out on Facebook about Steven and our request for riders to escort his coffin, the following Monday at his funeral.

I had a very disgruntled ex husband on the phone, saying had I seen the photos on Facebook? Paul, our son, had been jet-skiing in Dubai with his friends and he didn't think it was appropriate. I tried to explain that his friends were most probably trying to keep his spirits up, by doing something physical and keeping his mind off the fact that his brother had just recently died.

These past few years in Dubai, Steven and Paul had formed such a strong bond between each other and it was hard for Paul. He had remained strong last week for us and now obviously after our departure he was maybe not coping very well. I was grateful that his friends were looking after him but in any case life goes on and especially when you are twenty one.

Marion, my friend, came and sat with me until nearly midnight, then once she had left I went to bed.

Friday 19th August

Again I was up at the crack of dawn. It was 8:15 a.m. when I left the house today. I was wanting to get some photos of Steven printed. That's the thing these days, we have them all on our phones.

Afterwards, I went to have a coffee at the cafe in Marks and Spencer's and as I was sitting, a lady came and sat at the next table with her grandson. She was talking to him, telling him that his nana had died and had gone to Heaven. Then she started to sing to him. She was singing the same nursery rhymes which I used to sing to Steven. I broke down and cried, I was no good, I just had to get up and leave and get back to the car as soon as I could.

I got in the car and sobbed my heart out, my baby had gone, my gorgeous, gorgeous boy was no more. I cannot tell you what the pain in my heart felt like nor feels like still. It's as if someone had gotten hold of it and was tearing it apart. I decided to go back home, I was no good for anything today.

More visitors, more flowers and I now had one hundred and thirteen cards. I couldn't believe so many people were thinking about our loss. The continuous company, I was so grateful for, as I was truly finding it so hard to keep going when I was on my own. I have to admit that all the company wore me out but at least it helped me to sleep at night.

On the evening Marion and her partner Wayne arrived bearing gifts of fish and chips for us all. So we all sat around the kitchen table and enjoyed them.

Marion had successfully made the CDs for the funeral with a few spare for us and close friends. It was so thoughtful and generous of her to give her time up to do it for me, as she is such a very busy lady and such a wonderful friend.

Saturday 20th August

My friends Margaret and Stan came up from Sunderland today, to take me out for my lunch, everyone was being so kind. We went to our local Italian, Bon Appetito. I enjoyed the company and the meal was tasty and they encouraged me to eat.

When we came back to my house and were sitting having a coffee and talking about various topics, it cropped up in the conversation that Margaret's daughter's friend had just got the job as Manager at the local Harley Davidson's dealership in Gateshead.

I rang the dealership and they told me that they would indeed be coming to ride in the escort on Monday, for Steven's funeral.

The person I spoke to on the phone, Grant, had actually worked with Steven at Harley Davidson, Silverlink. He said he had actually been offered the job to go to work in Dubai but had said because he was married with two children, that Steven had been their man and that's how Steven had ended up in Dubai.

When my visitors left, I sat and listened to the CD of Steven's music. It gave me great comfort, as I could hear Steven singing the songs when we used to drive along in his car, in Dubai. We would sing them together.

Marion came and sat with me again on the night. I will be forever in her debt. I couldn't explain how grateful I was.

Sunday 21st August

Today I attended the 8:00 a.m. service, at our local church. I couldn't bare to attend the later service with the hymns, I was better just saying the prayers.

Afterwards my friend Anne came and took me for a walk along by the riverside. It was just what I needed, a bit of fresh air and some de-stressing at the same time.

We came back to mine for coffee and cake until it was time for me to leave to go to Newcastle Airport to pick Paul up. He was arriving on the Emirates lunchtime flight from Dubai, ready for Steven's funeral tomorrow.

Once I had picked Paul up, we stopped off on the way back for Sunday lunch. Paul was starving, he always is after his 7.5 hour flight.

We needed to go to the Metrocentre too, there were a few things Paul needed for Steven's funeral tomorrow. We did various other bits of running around and then it was midnight before we knew it and we fell into our beds exhausted yet again.

Monday 22nd August

I woke at 6:15 a.m., I sat in bed and read all of the lovely messages people had put on Facebook for me. I had, up until now, never liked Facebook but these past couple of weeks I have found it invaluable.

I got up, sat quietly, meditated then prayed. I prayed that God would give me the strength and anything else I may need to help me get through today, I needed Divine support.

I showered, dressed then made Paul and I a cooked breakfast, we needed something on our stomachs today. Then it was time to set off to go to his dad's, as that was where the funeral was leaving from.

Paul's dad's sister and her husband had already arrived when we got there, they had travelled down from Oban the previous day and had been staying at a local hotel.

I prepared everyone some lunch and as time was getting closer I had this awful feeling of dread come over me. It was like waiting to go to the gallows, it couldn't have been any worse.

At 12:45 p.m. the first bike arrived and they kept coming until there were thirty of them, my prayers had indeed been answered. Steven would have loved them.

The hearse arrived, being pulled by a Harley Davidson, it was time. The aunties and uncle were going to go in a different car but I said no they were to come with us and so we went to get into the funeral car.

One of the bikers, the one I had spoken to on the phone, with regards to organising the escort, came up to me and asked if I would like a 'bikers' salute.' I hadn't a clue what one was but decided to say yes. He said they would do it at the crematorium. I thought no more about it as I walked towards and got into the waiting funeral limousine, with the rest of the family.

The slow journey to the church began.

I was worried about how we were all going to stay together, with the everyday traffic but I need not have worried. Some of the riders had gone on ahead to stop all of the oncoming traffic, enabling everyone to keep together. It was absolutely amazing, even the driver of our car said he had seen nothing like it.

We arrived at church and got out, the priest came over to talk to me and I had to say to him that I couldn't take in anything of what he was saying. I was shaking so much. I began to panic, could I get through this? I just didn't know.

Paul came up to me and asked if he should ask his cousins if they would like to help him and his dad carry Steven's coffin. I said yes if he wanted to. He asked them and they all agreed they would. Steven would have so appreciated them doing that.

They started to make their way forward, the priest leading the way, then Paul, his dad, Michael, Nigel, Richard and Ben carrying Steven's coffin and I followed behind. I felt so alone, walking down that aisle, the relatives walking behind me. I couldn't look at anyone, I just had to focus on putting one foot in front of the other. I just kept telling myself, it wasn't Steven in the coffin, his spirit had left his body in Dubai, it was only his remains.

We sat in our seats and the service began. When it was time, the priest looked at me and gave me the prompt that it was time for me to go and read the eulogy. I had to do this, it was the last thing I could do for my precious son, as Steven's remains lay in the coffin on my left hand side.

I was okay once I started reading, until I was just nearing the end, as I was rounding up the eulogy, I turned and looked at the coffin and it was at that moment that I almost lost it. My voice broke, I paused, took a deep breath and then carried on to the end. I had done it.

I could not have let anyone else read it. I had brought Steven into this world and this was, as his mum, the last thing I could do for him. I delivered what I hope Steven would have wanted me to say. I hope I did him proud.

I returned to my seat and it was Paul's turn. He gave a wonderful speech about why his big brother was so special to him, he had even made it humorous in parts and had everyone laughing. I was so proud of him. His voice broke a couple of times but he did it and Steven would have been so proud of him, they loved each other so much. They were what 'brotherly love' was all about.

We sang Psalm 23, the priest said the final prayers then it was time to make our way back up the aisle. A friend reached out and touched my arm, showing me her love and support. As I came to the church door I tripped and if it hadn't have been for my sister Joy taking hold of my arm just seconds before, I would have fallen.

We got into the car and sat waiting until they got the coffin into the hearse. As I was sitting there, I noticed Dannielle, Steven's closest friend. I hadn't realised that she was in the U.K. I thought she was back in Dubai but apparently she was here on holiday. I got back out of the car to give her a big hug, I knew just how upset she would be.

Time to go, the congregation were all standing outside, waiting to see the bikers escort and hurse move off on Steven's final journey.

I was later told that no-one had seen anything like it, the roar of the bikes gave everyone goosebumps. (Joy said

196

they were talking about it in the village for weeks afterwards.)

We arrived at the crematorium, by this time it felt as though every organ in my body was shaking. I have never in my life experienced anything like it. I stood for what seemed like ages waiting. I couldn't understand what we were waiting for.

Everyone was standing just waiting for the coffin bearers to start carrying the coffin. They stood with the coffin resting on their shoulders and apparently I couldn't see but a very tall biker standing at the back, gave the 3,2,1 signal and the whole thirty bikers revved their bike engines, 'A Bikers' Salute.'

I cannot tell you what it was like, it touched your very soul and all I could think of was Steven would have absolutely loved it. He loved to be different and his funeral was definitely that, we had done him proud.

We slowly moved into the crematorium, apparently there were so many people that they were even standing at the back. All I could do was keep my focus straight ahead of me. That is until I saw Paul lift Steven's cap off the coffin and that was it, I was completely gone. I broke my heart, it was so final, Steven was no more. I cried all the way through the prayers then a peace came over me as we sat and watched Chris's presentation.

Afterwards we slowly made our way out, stopping to thank the priest for a beautiful service and we made our way to where the undertaker had laid Steven's flowers on the grass, in the beautiful hot summer sunshine.

There had been over three hundred and fifty people at his funeral, not all of them had come to the crematorium but those who had, had made their way afterwards to offer us their condolences and they all had commented on the presentation, saying how happy Steven had looked. It really had shown just how much Steven had loved his life in Dubai.

It was good that we had shown the presentation, as they had not seen Steven since he had moved to Dubai three years previously, on 1st January 2014. His much loved Nana Florrie had died just seven weeks after he left and he just couldn't face coming back when she wouldn't be there. We went out to see him instead.

It was all over. It had taken every morsel in my body to get through it. I was both physically and mentally exhausted. I hope I never have to go through anything else like it in my lifetime. I don't wish that on anybody, it is the hardest thing anyone could and does go through, loosing a child. These past three weeks had certainly taken its toll on me.

We headed off to the venue, a lot of people came back, each relaying to me their memories of Steven. I learnt a few things about him. One that stands out was from a friend of Danielle's who Steven had also been friendly with. She said she used to have an awful job until one day Steven had done her C.V. for her and now thanks to Steven, she had a wonderful job. Steven had been working quietly, unknown to others, changing people's lives. He had done what he had come here to do and now, job done, it was time for him to go back to his maker.

People drifted away and it was just his cousins Judith, Richard and their respective partners and a couple of our old staff from when we had had our hotel, before the divorce, who stayed behind and of course Paul, his dad and myself. We sat and talked about old memories, the staff remembering Steven as a young boy, when we would take him into work and he would help the staff with their jobs, Steven thinking he was boss. He had even told the chef he was sacked, at the age of six.

Someone said we had to have a toast to Steven and of course it had to be a Jack Daniels, Steven's favourite tipple, which we did. To be honest there may have been several. Then it was time to make our way home, some a little bit worse for wear, maybe it was their bodies just protesting after the ordeal of what they had been through these past sixteen days.

Paul asked me to stay at his dad's house, which I must say, I was very uncomfortable about doing but I would do anything for my boy. When we got back to the house Paul broke down and cried like a baby. He couldn't bare the fact that he wouldn't see his brother again. I don't think any of us can really.

The day had been just too much for Paul and maybe it was the alcohol which he had consumed but at least he was finally releasing the pain he was feeling and he wanted me there to comfort him and why not. He also had his close friend Ryan at his side.

It's hard to think, no more texts, Face time, group hugs, or big tight hugs as I stepped off the plane in Dubai, well at least not from Steven. I'll never see his fantastic smile, no more sarcasm, no more getting excited about Christmas. It's going to be very hard to bare.

I was just about to go to bed when his dad took me to one side and said could he ask me something. He asked me if Paul was indeed his son. I was shocked, astounded and taken aback that he could even think anything like this especially on the day we had just had our elder son's funeral. I told him that it was him who had had the affair not me!

What a way to end one of the worst days in my life but life goes on and we live to see another day.

Tuesday 23rd August

We were quite subdued at breakfast this morning, we sat and discussed the day before and how well it had all gone. But it was no good sitting around, someone at the funeral had come across to me to say that Steven and Paul's old school, Sunderland High School, had some framed photos of Steven and Paul and they would like us to have them.

There were also a few boxes with Steven's magic magazines and various other things, which I wanted to drop off to an old friend, who was still active in the Newcastle Magic Circle, where Steven in his younger day was a member of.

I said bye and went off to do these jobs. The school was actually packing up, as it was closing down but I managed to see the person who used to be Steven's form teacher, Mrs Robson, she told me that everyone was devastated by the news and offered their condolences.

I picked up what they had for us then went to drop the box of magic magazines off. This person lived quite close to the school.

Jobs done, I went back to Paul's dad's house, made some lunch and again we just sat and reminisced. After yesterday, it was very hard to face reality today. Steven was no more and we were trying our best to come to terms with it.

The past few weeks had kept us extremely busy but now it was all over, it was hitting us quite hard. We all felt extremely tired. The 'ex' went upstairs to bed, I lay on the settee and we all slept for a couple of hours. We certainly were all feeling exhausted today, yesterday had taken its toll on all of us.

However, today was another day and Paul was leaving tomorrow to go back to Dubai but before he did, we had to celebrate Paul's birthday, as on Thursday Paul would be twenty two, we couldn't let it go by without celebrating.

I went back home to Weardale to shower and change. Paul and his dad followed on behind, then once I was ready, we all went to Newcastle to Fujiyama, Paul's favourite restaurant when he's home in the U.K.

I was determined Paul should still celebrate his birthday. Steven would never have wanted Paul not to, as he used to love birthdays and Christmas.

What was strange was as we sat around the big table, in the restaurant, the guy sitting next to his dad was called

Steven. Was it Steven's way of letting us know that he was still with us? Maybe! Only now we just can't see him.

This was one of the many synchronicities that have occurred since Steven's passing.

It was very hard for all of us, none of us felt like celebrating but we had another son alive and we had to make an effort for Paul. It's strange how life goes on, everything changes, you have to adapt or get left behind. Life waits for no man, literally.

Thursday 25th August

It was hard saying goodbye to Paul at the airport today and sending him back to Dubai. Dubai where I had lost my elder son. I was very tearful as I gave him hug after hug, telling him how much I loved him. I could tell Paul was finding it hard to, normally as I stand at the bottom of the escalator watching him go up to security, he never looks back but today was different, he turned and looked back several times and waved. My heart went out to him.

I had to brainwash myself, I kept having to say over and over, Paul is alright, everything is okay and nothing is going to happen to him, he is safe and all is well. I now firmly believe that.

The ex drove me back to my little house in the country then he left and my life had to go on.

Friday 26th August

I got up today and actually felt okay, I felt as normal as I was going to feel, seen as it had only been four days since my son's funeral. I decided to do some housework.

Everything was going fine until I received a phone call from the ex, to say he was on his way to pick up Steven's ashes. We had already decided beforehand that I would pick them up. I got really upset then I thought just let it go, it's all about control and I won't let him control me anymore.

He wanted us to take turns every two weeks at having Steven's ashes. I said no because I felt it was not being respectful to Steven. Instead I suggested he have them for eight weeks and then I would have them for eight weeks, until such time Paul would be back in England and we could arrange the internment of Steven's ashes. After the phone call I felt myself spiralling down, I felt so restless and tearful.

I have to say at this point, I wasn't angry with God, I was grateful that He had taken Steven immediately and had not let him suffer. I can't even go there, if Steven had survived, he would have been quadriplegic and he would have hated that. Steven was a free spirit, happiest when he was out riding his bike in the desert. I couldn't wish him alive and suffering like that. I had felt that because everything had gone so smoothly up until now, I truly believe we had had Divine help, I listened and followed the directions I was given.

But something strange happened!

We had had a collection for three charities the day of Steven's funeral and had raised £850.00. This was being divided and shared equally between The Great North East Air Ambulance, Northumbrian Blood Bikes, and The British Bikers Foundation Trust. I was wanting to get it over the £1,000 and thought of selling Steven's Harley clothing and various memorabilia but I wasn't sure where would be the best place to sell them.

However, as I said, I was having a very bad day, I'd cried for most of it and if I had enjoyed having a tipple, I think I would have turned to the bottle, it was that bad.

I was sitting in my chair when a voice told me to go to the beach. I thought yes, I feel better when I go to the beach. So I decided I would go to Roker but again I was told no, not Roker, South Shields. Strange I always go to Roker. I asked again and I firmly got told that I needed to go to South Shields.

So I set out, Marion rang me as I was driving, so I stopped, pulled over and took her call. She was worried about me and especially because I could hardly talk to her, I was crying so much but I managed to get out that I was going to the beach and she agreed I always feel better when I am at the coast. So I said bye and went on my way.

My phone rang again, it was my great niece Megan, to say she had been to see a specialist at the hospital that day, but something strange had happened whilst she was sitting in the waiting room.

A lady who had been sitting beside her, said she was not a practicing Medium but she was learning to become one and she had a gentleman insistent she give Megan a message. Megan told her it would most probably be her grandad. The lady asked her if he had had his funeral on Monday of that week, to which Megan had said no, it was her cousin. Well she said he desperately wanted her to tell his family that he didn't want to go but he was happy!

When Megan told me this I felt a lot better knowing Steven was okay and that he was able to find some way of letting us know. A calmness came over me.

She also said that Steven had loved his funeral but also that he had had terrific pain in his head, neck and back when he died. He'd gone on to say that he hadn't passed over yet but he was happy and he had people with him. I was so delighted she had rang me, I thanked her then continued on my travels.

When I got to the sea front at South Shields, I parked beside Minchella's cafe, all of the bikers go there. I used to take the boys there when they were young. They used to love walking up and down the street admiring the various types of motorbikes parked up in front of the cafe.

I got myself a cup of coffee and sat outside, at one of the small bistro tables, as it was a very pleasant evening and I had brought my little dog, Alfie with me for company. Alfie also loves the seaside.

There I was, sat drinking my coffee, when I noticed a Harley Davidson pull up and a woman get off it. It's not very often you see a woman riding a Harley. So I waited until I had drank my coffee and then I went over to her. I explained to her how my son had died and I was wondering where would be the best place to sell his Harley gear, I was wanting to raise more money for the charities.

She said she knew just the person, if I gave her my details she would get in touch with this person and she was sure he would be in touch. She stood up, gave me a big hug and I went off to walk Alfie.

Well we hadn't been walking more than ten minutes when my phone rang. I answered it and the gentleman on the other end told me that his name was Paul, the guy the lady had told me about. I explained what I wanted to do and he said "Steve, who worked at Silverlink?" I said "Yes".

He said "He sold me my first bike, leave it with me, I'll get back to you."

I thanked him for getting in touch, then said goodbye. I finished walking Alfie along the beach before we made our way back to my car. I have to say, by which time I was feeling 100% better than when I had set out, knowing that this was the reason why I had to come to South Shields. Spirit was guiding me and I had listened and heard correctly.

This gentleman Paul, got in touch with me a few days later to say the President of the Geordie Chapter of the Harley Davidson Bikers had agreed to do an auction at their October meeting and he invited me and my friend Marion to go along for the auction, where hopefully we would raise more money and by doing so, help others and possibly save someone's life. So some good had come out of all of this.

And Life Goes On!

What I want to tell you about now are the many things which have happened since Steven died and how I know beyond a shadow of a doubt that he does indeed live on, I feel him near me, I can hear him at times and the synchronicities that have happened to show me that he is indeed with us still. I have already mentioned a few but I experienced a lot more and still do.

People can't believe how well I am coping but when you have faith, hope and love and know God is there for you, you can start to live your life again.

I firmly believe Steven's death was like an epiphany for me. I looked at what he had done, the eulogy I had given of the many things he had achieved in his short life. He never let money bother him, he wasn't materialistic, he just got on and lived his life to the full. As I sat and thought about it, I thought I cannot waste my life, sitting, moping and crying all of the time, I have to get on and live it.

Just before Steven died I had seen an advert for Hay House Writers Workshop which was going to be held in November 2016, in London. After Steven's funeral I rummaged about until I found the advert and because I had been writing a book, I decided to book a place and go along and find out more about it.

But first, I had already booked to go on a pilgrimage to the shrine at Walsingham. People were amazed that I was still going. I couldn't understand why they should think that way because where better to go for healing than to Our Lady of Walsingham when I felt the way I did.

Also the day before Steven died, Margaret had rung me and asked if I could go to Zante in October as she and a friend had booked it the night before but unfortunately the friend couldn't now go, could I take her place? I had rung to see if I could get Alfie minded and when I got the okay, I rang Margaret back to say yes and paid in full for the holiday. Was it meant to be? I think it was because no way would I have agreed to go once Steven had passed away.

Saturday 27th August

I attended Kynren, an historical event which is held in the grounds behind Bishop Auckland Castle. I felt sick and quite ill as the actors carried in coffins, all I could see in my mind, was Steven's face in one of them. They also played Silent Night and Steven hated Silent Night but I connected with it.

These I learnt are what our loved ones do, to enable us to realise that they are just a breath away. They send us signs which we connect with.

Sunday 28th August

I am sure Steven is communicating with me, I could hear a voice in my head and also my knees were icy cold. There was a presence near me.

On my way to taking Alfie to be groomed this morning, I had a flashback of Steven lying in his coffin. (Is this Post Traumatic Stress?) However, later when I was waiting outside for the groomer to finish Alfie, I couldn't believe it when a robin landed on my car wing mirror then went and sat on the fence and stared right at me. Is it a sign? I think so!

Later in the day, I went with my friend Sue to Hexham. We were sat in a coffee shop having a bite to eat when I suddenly realised that there across the Market Square, was a large white sign STEVEN. It was as if he was saying for goodness sake mum I am here, I am spelling it out for you. I had to smile.

Sue says she loves it when I get a sign because my face lights up.

Wednesday 31st August

I can't stop thinking about Steven lying dead on the road, in a pool of blood. I panicked, I wasn't sure which day Steven had died on, due to the time difference. Had we got the right day? I texted Steven's girlfriend, Ban and asked her. She confirmed that yes he had indeed died on the 6th August. Panic over.

I keep hearing a voice saying "I'm sorry, I'm sorry!"

SEPTEMBER

A friend gave me the telephone number of a Medium, who saw parents who had lost a child. I rang her and explained how I had just lost my son. She told me she could see me the next day. She asked me to take a friend with me to jot everything down, as I wouldn't be in any fit state to do so myself. This I did.

At first she said she might not get him through but immediately afterwards she said "He's here!"

My friend Sue wrote nine pages of A4 notes, it was so amazing and I had no doubt it was Steven, this too gave me so much comfort.

When the Harley Davidson Geordie Chapter got in touch to say they were having the auction on the 6th October, the day I was returning from Zante, I was so delighted. I couldn't help thinking Steven would think it was great, his mum going to a Geordie Chapter meeting.

Friday 2nd September

Almost a month after Steven's passing, I decided to take my bereavement cards down, all 130 of them. I felt quite melancholy. I must try and get on with my life. I sat for ages with all of them on my knee, holding them and having a few tears.

Saturday 3rd September

It's a month to the day since Steven passed, it feels like a lifetime.

Today I had to help out on the W.I. stall at the Wolsingham Annual Show. In my break I decided, even though it was tossing it down with rain, I would go outside the marquee and have a wander around.

The first thing I set eyes on was a coffin, the undertaker stand was directly opposite our marquee. I became quite tearful.

Then on the evening I sat and watched the X Factor, a girl came on and sang "With You" from the movie Ghost. I broke my heart.

So many connections, is this how it is going to be?

Sunday 4th September

I woke up from a dream, Steven was showing me that he was going along a road, then suddenly it went pitch black. Almost immediately a dazzling white light shone and I woke up. I just knew he had just shown me how quick he had died.

I went to church and twice the Psalm 23 was said and sung. The sermon was about the prodigal son and how God carried him home. I really felt that was for me today. I can feel Steven around me.

Tuesday 6th September

Today I struggled to get out of bed but I had to get up, Alfie needed his walk and so I got up and took him for his walk. Today we walked to the Demesne Picnic Area and along to the waterfall. I sat on the seat and as I talked to God, the tears started to fall.

Even when I went to the opticians later, I cried all the way there. It really was not a good day. Later in the day, as I walked Alfie in the afternoon, a butterfly flew beside me most of the way. This small thing really lifted my mood and then when I was driving to my meditation group, I could see a face in the clouds.

So many signs.

Wednesday 7th September

I felt I was coping a bit better today until I received a letter telling me when Steven's inquest was going to be. Then the ex called to say he had been looking at a plot in the churchyard where he thought Steven's ashes should go and then eventually when he died, his ashes would go in with them.

I said that this could not be so, as the three of us in Dubai had made the decision that Steven's ashes would go in the grave of his Nana Florrie, who Steven had adored and loved.

The ex told me that he had Steven's authority, which he did not have and then he told me that the church would not allow Steven's ashes to be put in the grave with his Nana's ashes.

213

He got rather nasty, I got upset. I couldn't deal with this, so I rang my eldest nephew, Michael, to ask if he would talk to him. Wrong move! I had given my power to someone else and I knew it as soon as the words had left my mouth.

I then rang the undertaker and explained what had happened and he said he would look into it for me.

As I was on the telephone, I could see a butterfly at the window, something was telling me that everything would be okay. I had texted Paul in Dubai and he rang me immediately, telling me that he would speak to his dad that day. The authority apparently his dad had, had been for any query to do with Steven's banking, whilst Steven was working in Dubai.

Paul wasn't long in phoning back to say that no way was Steven's ashes going into a different grave, they would be buried with his Nana Florrie.

I tried to calm down, I was so disappointed in myself for getting upset. I knew I should have just given the situation up to God and all would be sorted for the highest good.

Friday 9th September

This weekend I was on my pilgrimage to Walsingham. It was good to be back amongst old friends, I felt safe and comforted.

The journey was fine and the first set of prayers went well, when we arrived. A peace came over me, there is something very magical about this place, it is so spiritual, you can feel it as soon as you walk into the grounds. I think it's my eighth time I have been.

We had been shown our accommodation and Gill who I always share with and myself were totally surprised, as we had been given a cottage just outside of the shrine, what an amazing place it was. God was looking after us.

After supper we went into church and waited for the Intersessions which were going to be held in the Holy House. As I was sitting waiting, I suddenly felt a featherlike kiss on my cheek. It was the most beautiful thing I have ever experienced. It felt wonderful.

Unfortunately, as we prayed for the departed including Steven, I got very upset. The curate, who had been present at Steven's funeral, came and put his arm around me to comfort me. The heat that came from him, was like a healing heat. I was safe and in the perfect place to bring my grief to God.

Saturday 10th September

After breakfast we were meeting at 10:00 a.m. for The Stations of the Cross. We had to do them inside today, the first time ever when I have been there but the rain was coming down in buckets and no way could we do it outside in the grounds.

Whilst we were doing the Stations, I found myself getting upset, especially when Mother Mary held Jesus' broken body, I thought back to when I was sitting in the back of the truck, in Dubai, when I had laid Steven's stiff, blood stained leather waistcoat on my knee and I had felt as if Steven was lying with his head on my knee for one last time. Mother Mary knew my pain!

Sunday 11th September

After breakfast Gill and I went to Reception to purchase a seven day candle which I took to the Holy House, lit it and it would burn for the next seven days. I also filled in a request to have Steven's name included in the Intersessions and during the service I asked and prayed for healing.

I gave thanks to God for allowing me to be Steven and Paul's mum and for giving me twenty nine very precious years with Steven and hopefully a lifetime with Paul. I was very honoured to be their mum and gave thanks for the many lessons Steven had taught me.

Our priest had arranged for our Morning Eucharist to be in the Barn Chapel, which we all love. One of our priest's dear friends, who is also a priest was going to take the service as it was his last service before he retired.

Well we laughed, we cried, we linked arms and swayed as we sang joyous hymns and at the end of the service, tears of both sadness and joy were rolling down each and everyone's cheeks. It was so special, I can't tell you just how much.

By 4:00 p.m. that afternoon, I felt I had done everything I could and I gave thanks to God for taking good care of both my precious boys, one in Heaven and one on

Earth, more tears as we sang the farewell hymn, it just gets you, well it gets me every year.

It was time to go, with a very teary farewell, we all got back on the bus, ready for our journey home. Until next year, God willing!

You need to visit the Walsingham shrine, to understand just how special it is. I feel I plug in and get charged up, ready to go out and live my life for another year. The atmosphere on the bus travelling back each year is euphoric.

Thursday 15th September

Today, was a beautiful sunny day, too nice to stay indoors and so I took myself off to Hill End by the stream. Steven and Paul used to love to come here when they were small for a picnic with me and their nana. They would play in the stream and climb the trees.

But today, none of that, I had brought my pen and jotter and I positioned my director's chair close by the stream, I sat and wrote whilst around me families were enjoying their picnics and having fun just like what we used to do. Such happy memories.

I could even remember sitting in the car, watching Steven playing in the stream, I hadn't known it then but I was actually in the first stages of labour with Paul. Paul had been born by Caesarean section the next morning.

When I got back home, on the night, whilst sitting in the lounge I decided to watch the girl on X Factor singing 'With You.' I had recorded it, because it was so beautiful but maybe I shouldn't have watched it, as I broke down and cried again. I feel I keep my emotions under lock and key and it takes something like this song to open the flood gates.

Friday 16th September

I received a telephone call today from the undertakers, they had done a memorial book and they wanted my okay on it. Inside it, they had printed the church service, some poems, copies of the cards which had been on the wreaths and some photographs of motorbikes, unfortunately they were sports bikes and not Harley Davidsons.

I explained that if I was going to order any, then I would have to have the bikes changed. I requested that they change them for Steven's logo of his business Hustle Cycles and put a photograph of his custom built Harley Davidson, Steven had built it himself, his Black Betty.

After going through the memorial book, the undertaker went on to inform me that the church would not allow us to bury Steven's ashes in his Nana Florrie's plot but he had been to the graveyard, taken a photograph of the plot behind his Nana's grave and showed me the plot on his mobile phone.

Something in my gut was telling me this was not so and so when I left the undertakers, I went and purchased some flowers and took them to my mum's grave. I put the flowers in a vase and stood and asked God, that if Steven had not to go beside my mum then so be it but if he was to go beside her, then please could He help me.

Again something told me to knock on the local priest's door and ask his advice. I went and knocked on the vicarage's door and his wife answered, she said the priest wouldn't be long and when he arrived at the door I explained the situation. He said "Of course he can go with his Nana, that would be where I would expect your son to go."

I had just known they had been telling me lies.

The priest told me to bypass the undertaker and he gave me the telephone number of the stonemason and said for me to do it myself and he and the priest who was doing the service would sort out about the service and the actual internment of Steven's ashes.

I could not believe that the undertaker would do such a despicable thing. I was like a woman on a mission. I spoke to the stonemason, got the necessary details then called back at the undertakers.

The gentleman I spoke to that morning was not available but I saw the gentleman who had done my mother's funeral. I explained how deeply upset I was that they were not carrying out the original wishes and he was shocked to think I had actually gone and knocked on the vicarage's door. I think he thought I would have taken their word for what would happen.

He did not realise that he was dealing with a mum who would go to the end of the earth for her sons and Steven would have not wanted to go anywhere other than with his Nana Florrie.

The undertaker rang me later and apologised.

I truly learnt today, to go with your gut feeling, if you don't think something is right, do not go along with it.

That night, the treasurer of the Geordie Chapter came to collect Steven's Harley Davidson memorabilia and clothing, they were doing the auction at the next meeting.

Monday 19th September

I received several texts from the ex today to say

"Be it on your conscience, if you go ahead and bury Steven's ashes with his nana."

The ex had obviously gone to see the vicar whose graveyard Steven's ashes were being buried in and he had also visited the priest who was going to be doing the internment.

The priest who was going to do the internment contacted me to say no way could he go ahead with the internment until this sorry mess was sorted. He needed the ex to agree.

This was just what I needed when I was desperately trying to cope with the death of my boy. I sat and prayed and hoped God would find a solution.

Tuesday 20th September

I woke at 4:20 a.m. Paul was messaging me from Dubai. I was really worried about him, he was upset because his dad wouldn't agree to what the three of us had already agreed to. I said I was so sorry, we had to involve him but he was Steven's brother and he did have a say.

When I got up at 8 a.m. I sat and prayed and asked God for guidance.

Later that morning I had word from the priest to say he would be mediator if it would help sort this mess out, he was really nice about the whole thing. I contacted Paul to keep him informed and he seemed relieved.

Apparently Paul had also contacted his friend Ryan, who had been to see his dad the night before and Ryan had told his dad just how much Steven had loved his Nana. So fingers and everything else crossed, everything is working out. Thank you Lord.

Saturday 24th September

After breakfast I walked Alfie to the waterfalls and sat on the seat which overlooked them. I had these words going round and round in my head "I don't want to be here but I'm fine."

Had it really been Steven's time or had he been taken too soon? The tears started to fall and just wouldn't stop. I will never know but what I do know is, it's devastating. Alfie and I sat for ages then we walked home.

Sunday 25th September

I woke after a very disturbed night, I had been dreaming that I had been in Dubai, in some very seedy places trying to piece together Steven's life.

It effected me all day, as strange dreams do. I have an awful feeling of dread and it won't go away.

Monday 26 September

I received a text from Ban today to say Steven's dad had contacted her with regards to Steven's ashes. She then rang me. Of course, she is a Muslim and in their religion the man dominates.

I explained what he was trying to do. She agreed that what we were doing was actually what Steven would have wanted, as he loved his Nana so much. I couldn't believe it when Ban said that his dad had told her that Steven was his and Paul was mine. Excuse me, I had given birth to two sons, neither of which I own as such and I love both my sons equally.

I cried all morning, how could he say such a thing, it was despicable.

This afternoon I went to see the Medium, for a second visit. She had told me to go back after a month, when Steven would be stronger. My friend Sue came with me again to be the scribe.

The Medium told me that Steven had sussed it out, it was Quantum Physics, he had been brilliant at Physics when he was at school, so I quite believed what she said. He said he didn't need her, he can come through me and

222

had been doing so, which I said confirms that when I had heard the voice, it was indeed Steven.

She talked to me for two hours, may I add without taking a fee, she would not take from parents who had lost their child. The things she told me, could have only been Steven, she even mentioned his friend Chris, who had done the presentation for the memorial service and she said how Chris came from America, which he did. She told me Steven's Nana had come to get him when he passed and I felt so much better knowing she was with Steven, taking care of him.

We left and I thanked her very much, it had been a great help to me. Sue took me to Whitworth Hall for our tea and it was only as I was eating my meal, that I remembered how I used to go there quite a lot, when Steven was little, with my mum and family friend Valerie and Steven. We would take a picnic and eat it in the grounds, which Steven had loved, as he also enjoyed roaming around and watching the deer.

That night, as I was going through some paperwork I came across a letter I had written to Steven in the eventuality of my death. It's really sad to think he hasn't been able to read it or has he? Can he see things in Spirit? I hope so. I hope he was looking over my shoulder.

Tuesday 27th September

I woke early today, with Steven on my mind. His songs ever present in my head, playing over and over.

Tomorrow is the meeting with the priest, my stomach was churning already. I had to stay positive and know that whatever happened, it would be for the highest good. What I did know was Steven would guide us to do what he wanted us to do.

Wednesday 28th September

Well I attended the meeting, I think the ex thought I had taken control which I suppose in hindsight I may have done, but if I had not been deceived there would have been no need.

First the ex spoke then I had my say then the priest wound up the meeting. We got through everything and it's how it has to be, Steven's ashes are to be buried in his Nana Florrie's grave at 11 a.m. on 23 December 2016, when Paul will be back in the U.K.

We were just about finished the meeting when the ex demanded I sign an agreement to say that if I died within the next six years, my ashes would not go into my mum's grave. The priest said there was no need for that.

We left the meeting and I went to the ex's house to pick up Steven's ashes, it was my turn to have them.

Thursday 29th September

Today was an extremely early start. I had to be up at 1:30 a.m. I was going on holiday with my friend Margaret, to Zante.

You might think it was far too soon after Steven's passing to be even considering going away but I had only booked and paid for this week away, the morning before Steven had passed over.

Something was telling me after Steven had died that it had to be, I had to go, why else would I have booked it there and then.

When we arrived at the hotel and found our room, I was amazed to find that above our beds was painted up the wall and over the ceiling, the picture depicting 'Footsteps in the Sand.' I just knew I had to be there, no-one else we spoke to had this above their beds.

We unpacked then decided to go and explore. The beach was only a five minute walk away and as we approached it, I noticed Dragonflies everywhere.

I had been told by the Medium, that when I saw Dragonflies, Steven was letting me know he was there, well he certainly was doing that.

I realised the reason why I had had to come was because each day we just walked to the beach and lay there under an umbrella until 6 p.m. each night, just as the sun was beginning to set. It was lovely and warm under the umbrella, and I lay there listening to the gentle ripple of the waves, it was all very therapeutic. The whole experience was very healing and relaxing.

OCTOBER

Monday 3rd October

Well it was relaxing, that is until I woke up on the Monday morning at 5 a.m. to feel my bed shaking. Margaret slept through it and didn't believe me when I informed her the next morning, as we were getting ready to go to breakfast, that I thought that there had been an earthquake during the night.

Later in the day, we were sitting around the pool, watching the sun go down, when Margaret overheard a conversation from people who were sat near to us. They were talking about the earthquake and how they had had to get out of their beds and go on to their balconies. Apparently it had measured 4.8 on the richter scale but because our room was situated on the ground floor, we hadn't felt it as badly as the people on the third floor.

Tuesday 5th October

I felt very tearful today, tomorrow we were leaving to fly home and I had this awful feeling of dread. Reality was kicking in. It had felt as though I had stepped off the world for a week but now I had to prepare to go back home knowing that it all hadn't just been a nightmare. My boy really was no more.

The masseuse came along the beach and I treat myself to a full body massage, I thought it might help to ease the tension. I have to say it was a very good massage and the added bonus was I could hear the waves lapping up onto the shore and smell the sea air.

Wednesday 6th October

Our last morning, we were getting picked up at 11 a.m. to be taken to the airport but before we did, I just wanted to go for one last walk along the beach. The tears started to roll down my cheeks. I really didn't want to go home. Whilst I have been here I could pretend that all was well and Steven was still working in Dubai.

When we later arrived back in Newcastle, I picked up my car and took Margaret home, to Sunderland. I then had to go to the ex's, he was wanting to put Steven's memorial in the Book of Remembrance at the crematorium and needed a letter from me to say that I agreed to him doing so.

I didn't think there was a need, as Steven's ashes were going to be interned and we would be able to visit his grave. He was insistent that we do it but could only go ahead, if I gave him my authority. He had made a point in telling me that he would include me in the memorial when we had been in the meeting with the priest.

So I wrote the letter, once we got back to Margaret's house and I dropped the letter off at his home. I had agreed to meet back up with Margaret and her family afterwards at the local pub for a meal.

Tonight I was meeting Marion, she was coming with me to the Geordie Chapter of the Harley Davidson's where they were going to auction Steven's Harley items.

You may wonder why I didn't invite the ex to go. Well the reason being was that he wanted everything for himself and wouldn't have allowed people to buy the items. They were bikers, his dad was not and he had a lot of items already. He had kept the large print of Steven from the memorial service and he also asked for the large picture of Steven and myself which the school had given to me, not to mention Steven's laptop and lots of other items. So I felt they were best going to bikers, as I said before, I was trying to do, what Steven would have wanted me to do.

At 7:15 p.m. I met Marion in the car park of the Nissan's Social Club, where she was waiting with Paul, the gentleman I had first spoken to, on the phone the day I had gone to South Shields. We went upstairs in the Social Club and I was amazed when I walked into the room, there must have been between 80-100 people already there, men and women, all bikers.

They welcomed us, and once we had got a drink we were shown to our seats. At 7:30 p.m. they started the auction. £445.00 was raised, which included a £20 donation.

The total we had raised now was £1,321.65. I was over the moon. What a day it had been!

(When I posted how much we had raised in total, on Steven's Facebook page, one of the dads from Go-Karting saw it and donated the remaining amount to make the total up to £1,500.00, which meant each of the charities got an equal share of £500.00.)

Sunday 9th October

Whilst I was out on the afternoon taking Alfie for his walk, I saw a beautiful rainbow. Afterwards I decided to have a nap, I was feeling very tired.

Well I woke with such a start, I could hear Johnny Cash's song 'God's Gonna Cut You Down.' Straight away I jumped up, thinking Steven was there!

The music was being played on an advert on the T.V. There was a rainbow on the screen and then a guy appeared on the advert on the T.V. with a welding mask on, just like on the short video I have of Steven welding. Again I thought he is well and truly letting me know he is with me. I really find these signs very comforting.

Sunday 16th October

I was having a sort out today and came across some gifts I had already bought and put away, ready for Steven's birthday and Christmas. I sat and broke my heart. It's so hard.

Once the rain had stopped, the reason why I was having a good sort out in the first place, I took Alfie for a long walk. I find getting out and being amongst nature is quite therapeutic, I walk and talk to God.

Monday 17th October

I was still feeling very tearful, so I kept myself busy, cleaning out cupboards all day long. I am finding it is better if I keep myself busy and the bonus is I am getting rid of lots of things I no longer need. So the thought that someone, somewhere, could put them to good use, was making me feel a bit better.

Tuesday 18th October

All day I had had a feeling of doom and gloom. Paul messaged me to say that he was in Italy, racing, and they were very close to Vesuvius.

Apparently the area had been put on red alert as the volcano had become active.

Brilliant, just what I didn't need to know. So I took myself upstairs, lit a candle and prayed to God, putting the volcano and Paul's safety in God's hands. I sat and shed a few tears. Every little thing seemed to panic me at the moment.

Thursday 20th October

A friend called today to tell me that they had just found out that her husband was dying of cancer. She said she needed me to get her through it.

I found this very difficult, as how can you prepare someone for what they have to go through? It didn't help that I was already having a bad day.

I had found some of Steven's things which he had brought back from Malawi, when he had been out there on a World Challenge with his school, when he was sixteen.

Friday 21st October

I broke down today when I was out and about. I couldn't help myself, it just came over me like a tsunami. The assistant in the shop was very understanding and gave me a big hug.

I am finding everything so, so hard. How do you carry on? I never know when it is going to come over me. It's like I said, a tsunami and I have no control over it. When the tears start I just have to go with it until a calmness comes over me.

I had called at the local nurseries to pick up my hanging baskets which were being refilled with winter bedding plants and I caught my eye on a big turquoise plant pot with a dragonfly on it, I just had to buy it.

Dragonflies seem to be cropping up all over the place. I do find it very comforting when I see one, whether it is a real one, a piece of jewellery or a picture. As soon as I see it, I think Steven is with me, he's here!

My therapy today was helping my friend Anne, pick her Quinces and apples. We spent an hour in her orchard and picked two huge baskets of each. Afterwards we went indoors and enjoyed a lovely cup of coffee and a piece of tea loaf before we went and had a brisk walk.

She lives high up, above Wolsingham and the views are spectacular.

I thank God every day for putting me in such a wonderful, healing place. If it wasn't for the loss of my boy, I would say that I had won the lottery of life. Simple and surrounded by nature. Perfect!

The decorator finished today, he had been painting the whole of the inside of my house, hence the reason for sorting out. I just needed to get some positive energy into the house. Having the decorator in had been so exhausting, I had to be up very early each day, enabling me to walk Alfie and be back home in time for the decorator starting. I emptied the room the night before which he was going to paint, then he would paint it. Once the paint was dry that night, I had to put everything back and then prepare the next room.

After he had done three rooms, I said I had to have a few days break as I was exhausted and then he could start again.

Today I was so delighted because he was totally finished, all done. I could now have a well earned rest. There were still lots of jobs for me to do but tonight I gave myself permission to sit in front of the T.V. and watch the fund raising for Cancer Research U.K. which maybe was not such a good idea, as I cried all the way through the programme.

Saturday 22nd October

As Alfie and I, were out walking today, I could hear an owl in the woods. I noticed the river was starting to rise, the wind had a cold chill to it and there was another rainbow in the sky. (I've seen a lot lately, another sign from Heaven.) The leaves were changing colour and falling fast. Winter was just around the corner. Time was passing so quickly.

That night, as I went to bed I received a text from Shabs, Steven's friend, who works for Emirates airlines. It said that he had managed to change his shift and would be flying into Newcastle the following Saturday. Could I meet him?

I was so surprised and delighted that one of Steven's friends would go to such lengths to come and see me.

Sunday 23rd October

Today I received a text from Paul to say he was safely back from Italy and was now in Dubai. I heaved a sigh of relief. Thank you Lord.

Monday 24th October

I had an appointment with my G.P. I felt I was not coping very well. Was this normal? I just didn't know. I was in with her for thirty minutes.

When I got home I started to look for some money I had safely put away whilst the house was upside down.

233

(It had safely been put away alright, I never found it until July 2017.)

I realised that when you are suffering from grief your mind plays tricks with you. It also shuts down if there is something which is too much for you to cope with. This has happened on several occasions and I had to step down from being Events Organiser at my local Women's Institute. I needed to just focus on me and getting through each day.

Thursday 27th October

Today I cried all of the time, whilst I was out walking with Alfie. When I got home I realised I had had a text from my friends to say meet them at No.10, our local coffee shop for a coffee and a catch up. I went and I have to say by the time it was time to leave I was feeling so much better.

I decided, as I was sorting Paul's room out, I wanted a new carpet for it. I took myself off to Stanhope, which is six miles away, to our local carpet fitters. I walked in the door and their before my very eyes was the exact carpet I was looking for. The Angels were indeed helping me in lots of ways.

Whilst there I decided to take Alfie for a walk along by the river, as it is one of mine and Alfie's favourite walks. We were literally walking on a bed of multi-coloured leaves and the squirrel had obviously been very hard at work, as there were lots of pieces of conkers scattered around. He must be preparing for winter.

I felt a little brighter, I had managed to get my jobs done and now the house was looking lovely, newly decorated and all sorted. The work had made me very tired but at least I was sleeping as soon as my head hit the pillow each night.

I think the fact that I had cleared out a lot of things and was feeling so much more organised I felt it was starting to have a healing effect on me.

Yes, I was maybe having bouts where I sat and broke my heart but at least I was getting it all out of my system. One day it had to get better. I don't suppose I will ever get over the fact of loosing my boy but if I can learn to live with it, he will be forever in my heart, that I do know.

Friday 28th October

Over these past months I have realised I have a terrific support system. Whatever I have needed doing, my friends have been there to help me.

Just like today, I had all the old carpet and rubbish from the decorator to dispose of and my friends Jeanette and Geoff arrived to take it all to the tip. I was so grateful.

Saturday 29th October

Today's the day Shabs is arriving in to Newcastle Airport for a twenty four hour turn around. I was picking him up at the Marriott Hotel, at the Metrocentre, Gateshead, an hour after the taxi had dropped the crew off. He was going to have a quick shower and change, then I would meet him at 1 p.m.

I was looking forward to seeing him. I hadn't seen him in Dubai to say goodbye to him. He was feeling too poorly to make it to Steven's memorial night.

It was the first time he had flown in to Newcastle, normally he works on the larger Emirates planes which are too big to land into Newcastle. He was amazed to see all of the surrounding green fields when they came in to land.

After I picked him up, I took him on the A68 to Corbridge where we stopped for a bite to eat before continuing on to Wolsingham. I was laughing at him, as he had not seen black cows and was taking photos of them, as I drove. He took lots of photos to show his family when he got back to Dubai. One thing he found it hard to grasp was the many shades of green in the countryside.

He actually made me see things differently, what I would maybe accept as normal were being presented to me in a different light.

When we got to my house, we sat and talked and talked about Steven. It was lovely having someone who knew him, who I could talk to.

What I also found funny, was my house phone rang just as we were about to leave and he couldn't believe we still had landlines. We got into the car and as I drove through the town he asked me "Where are all the children?"

236

There were no children playing outside. I said they would be all on their computers in their homes. He was shocked.

I dropped him back off at his hotel and said goodbye and thanked him for coming to see me. It really had been a lovely day and if I am honest it was like having a bit of Steven there with me.

Monday 31st October

All Souls' Day, the priest had invited us to go to the service at the church where we had had Steven's funeral, Steven's name would be amongst the many that they would be praying for.

My sister had asked if I minded if the ex come and sit with us in church. I didn't but I don't suppose it would have made any difference if I had. Joy and I walked into church and I was greeted by my old friends but my eye caught a glimpse of the ex in the background, waiting for us to arrive and his face was like thunder.

Brilliant, just what I needed.

I just rose above it, spoke to both him and my sister- in-law, Judith then moved to the pew where Gill and Roy were keeping our seats. At least I didn't have to sit next to him, as I had Gill on one side and Joy on the other.

It was a lovely service but as it finished, the ex hovered at the end of the pew and demanded Steven's ashes and his death certificate. I had neither of them with me.

Throughout October and November I was travelling back and forth to Fulwell in Sunderland twice a week, to go to the chiropractor. My lower back was giving me a lot of pain.

In hindsight I realised it wasn't just the chiropractor doing the healing, because every visit, I would take Alfie with me and after I had had my treatment, I would take Alfie down to the beach for a brisk walk. This in itself, I realised was very healing.

NOVEMBER

The beginning of November found me knocked for six with a sickness bug. I had to rest up as my body wouldn't allow me to do anything else. Maybe my body was telling me I had tried to do too much!

Sat 5th November

Today I must put all of my energies into what I want in my life and NOT waste it, on looking back at what has been. As of today, I am going forward to achieve my goals and dreams and I am not letting anyone stop or hinder me. I CAN DO IT! and I WILL! Onwards and upwards.

I will also pull back on what I give to people. I give too much of myself. Something is telling me to not give my all.

I started sorting through all of my family photographs. I was wanting to make an album for Paul titled 'My

Brother And Me.' I also wanted to make one for Ban showing her Steven's life before she had met him.

I had a really busy day as I also spent time sorting out paperwork, photocopying and whilst I was on, I printed out my travel documents, as yes I was off again.

I sat and asked myself why was I overweight and I decided that I hijacked my weight because if I was overweight then no man would find me attractive. I think I was pressing the self destruct button.

I went on to Facebook and Stairway to Heaven popped up, Steven keeps letting me know he is here. I ordered his gravestone and also 30 memorial books, to give to Paul, his aunty and cousins and all the Warpigs and of course Ban. I want them to have a keepsake. The ex would, I presume be ordering his own.

More clearing out and more treasured memories found. Steven's name tag from when he was born, letters he had wrote to me when he was little telling me how much he loved me and lots more.

I felt sad to think that in my Memory Box there was my dad, mum, my brother Cecil and now Steven. It's a huge loss.

Monday 7th November

I actually made a proper meal for myself today but still couldn't bare socialising. I felt better in my own space.

I apologised to the Supper Club and I knew nothing until there was a knock on my door. Mark the owner of No.10, where I go to the Supper Club was standing on my doorstep, with my dinner, dessert and a large glass of wine in his hand and one of the members was behind him, giving him a hand. He said I needed to eat and he had brought me my supper. I was so grateful and thankful for such a kind thought.

Unfortunately I could not eat it but I knew someone who would welcome it, my neighbour, a single mum of two. She would feed the kids and forget about herself. I texted her to say that her tea was ready if she would like to come in. Well she was delighted, she drunk the wine and thoroughly enjoyed the meal. She was so grateful for the meal and I was so grateful for the company. It was a win, win situation.

I had spent my day continuing with my sorting out. During my sort out, I came across a little book I had written on divorce. As I sat and read it, under all the layers I realised that the hurt and pain were still there, even though I have forgiven both myself and my ex.

Will it ever go? Who knows!

I seem to be doing a lot of crying. I am crying for the world it seems but I also seem to be getting angry at people because they just don't seem to understand what I am going through. They are comparing Steven's death to an ageing parent or a sibling. Loosing your child is nothing like that.

I have lost both parents and a brother who I loved dearly but now I have lost my boy and he was part of me. His egg grew inside of my body, I nurtured it, fed it, watered it and lovingly cared for it until such time Steven was born. It had been just the two of us for nine months then I had to share him with the world.

Nothing on Earth can prepare a mother for such a huge loss. He was part of me and always will be.

Saturday 11th November

This morning I received a beautiful bouquet and a box of chocolates from my dear friend Debra. She had phoned earlier in the week and I was crying so much I couldn't actually manage to talk to her. These thoughtful gestures are what keeps me going and I am so grateful to each and every one.

I also had a visitor, who said he had heard that I wasn't coping and then he went on to say "Life must go on."

Thank the Lord I had answered the door in my dressing gown, so it wasn't appropriate to invite him in. When he left I felt so angry, I went upstairs and wrote all of my feelings down. Yes I do know life goes on but it doesn't stop the tears from falling and my heart from breaking.

How can he possibly know what it feels like for a mother to loose her child. And yet the day before when I was at the chiropractors, I had burst into tears and

Peter, the chiropractor, came to me and gave me a big hug and said "I think you need one of these today."

Later that day I read what I had written earlier and I couldn't believe it had been me who had written it.

It had been a bad morning, so much so, that when I was walking Alfie, the tears dripping off my chin, I was forced to knock at my friend Pat's door, I felt desperate. Immediately she set eyes on me, she told me to go in and she asked her hubby John, if he would make me a cuppa. It took me an hour to compose myself, I felt awful but she said she was pleased I had felt the need to knock and told me any time, she was there for me. I left feeling a lot calmer and able to cope.

Adam, Steven's best friend in Dubai, was arriving into Newcastle today and so I had to get my act together as I was picking him up later. He too, like Shabs, had swapped his shift, to come and see me. He is a pilot with Emirates Airlines.

I was shocked at how many of Steven's friends were pilots for Emirates Airlines and what wonderful people they were too. Adam was also staying at the Marriott Hotel. I picked him up and took him where he could have a substantial meal, which was at the South Causey Arch Hotel. I had a child's portion but Adam being a big guy, enjoyed one of their speciality dishes. Adam must be about 6' 7" I am surprised he fits in the cockpit, needless to say, it takes a lot to fill him.

I have to say, I was a little apprehensive about meeting Adam, I didn't really get to see him other than when he picked us up at the airport, the night Steven died. He also came with the group of friends when they came to pay their respects and lastly at Steven's memorial but each time, I didn't get the opportunity to speak to him on a one to one basis. Here I was entertaining him for six hours.

Why had I worried, he loved the countryside and as we drove along we constantly spoke about Steven or as the guys called him Steve-O. We had a wonderful day together. When the time came to drop him back off at the hotel, he asked if I would text him, to let him know that I was home safely. He was very concerned about me driving home alone, along the dark country roads. I thought what a lovely, caring guy.

One thing Adam had mentioned whilst we had been talking was that when Adam had received the phone call from Ban, to say Steven had died, Adam, who only lives minutes away from where the incident occurred, had gone to the scene of the accident. When he arrived he saw the police dragging Steven's body out from underneath a car. Steven's crash helmet had split in two and was lying on the ground. My poor boy would never have known the death he died. It also explained to me why there was only one shoe in the blue plastic bag. The other must have come off at the scene of the incident, and had been left on the road.

We never got his watch or mobile phone, we presumed that they had been shattered on impact.

Tuesday 14th November

Today I decided to take myself off to Number 10 for lunch and I also had the dishes to return to Mark. As soon as I had put a foot in the door, Mark came over and gave me a big hug.

After I had had my lunch he wouldn't let me pay for my lunch and instead he gave me a takeaway box with some cake in for later. I so appreciated his generosity and kindness.

If there's anyone reading this who never knows what to do when they meet a person, who is grieving, give them a hug. You don't need to speak, just show them that you care, then you can talk about anything in general just don't ignore the fact that they have lost a loved one.

I was feeling very lethargic and tired today and when I feel like this I find meditating very helpful.

I was still getting abusive texts from the ex. Why won't he stop??? I didn't reply to them as I felt it would feed the fire, so to speak.

I have had several dreams about Steven of when he was little. Is he telling me to remember the happy times? I think so.

This week I have learnt from a posting on Facebook, how to convert your VHS tapes to DVD and so I packed them all up and took them to Tesco Superstore in Durham. It was expensive to get them done but honestly can you put a price on a memory of your loved one. For me the answer has to be no. Your memories are priceless.

(I still haven't been able to watch them, but one day hopefully I will!)

Friday 18th November

Today I set off on another adventure, this time I was off to London, to the Writers' Workshop. I saw it advertised and booked it after Steven had died.

I boarded the train at Durham but we hadn't gone far, Doncaster to be exact, when the train stopped. It wasn't long before it came over the tannoy that someone had jumped in front of a high speed train on another track and all trains had to stop until they got the all clear.

I felt physically sick, I thought of the person who had jumped, their family who would be getting the devastating news and would have to go through what I have and then there was the poor train driver, how will that effect him mentally? Total devastation!

After a while, we got on our way and after getting into London, I got a taxi to my hotel. I checked in, went to my room which I must say I was not satisfied with but thought I wasn't going to spoil my day and so unpacked and went to find a taxi to take me to Covent Garden. I love Covent Garden and Steven did too.

Well I got there, I wandered about but I was surrounded by people who were with their families on holiday. It was very cold and a really dark, damp, November day and after I had had a coffee and a little retail therapy I decided to get a taxi and have the driver take me to somewhere near to the Dominican Theatre, where I had a ticket to see The Bodyguard that night.

I asked the taxi driver if he could recommend anywhere to eat and he was just telling me to go down this side street when he pulled up at Garfunkels. My mum's favourite restaurant in London. I thanked him and went in to the restaurant and found a table.

The service was slow but I was not in a hurry, so I sat and people watched until my meal came. I still had time to spare when I came out and so I wandered along the street, found a wonderful bookshop, just what I love and spent the rest of the time browsing. I bought a couple of presents ready to put away for Christmas. So quite content with my purchases, I made my way back to the theatre, found my seat and sat down.

You know the feeling, you see some people and think are they coming to sit in front of you and if they are, please, please, please let the smaller of the two sit in front of me. Well unfortunately the very tall gentleman decided to sit in front of me. I have to say I am five feet two inches tall.

I thought if only he would swap with his partner, I would be able to see beautifully. Well what do you know, a couple of minutes later they swapped seats! Thank you Angels!

All through the performance I kept thinking of the time when Steven had been working in London, as a magician, in Hamleys Toyshop.

One Friday he had been sent home suffering from food poisoning when he had collapsed on one of the platforms in a tube station. They had to phone for an ambulance and have him taken to hospital.

When he eventually was able to contact me, to tell me what had happened, I caught the very early train the next morning, to go and see him. He came to meet me, his face looking a not very healthy shade of green.

When he was feeling a bit better, the following day, we went to see We Will Rock You, the musical. Steven had loved it and we had had a lovely time together.

Well when The Bodyguard finished, I came out of the theatre and as I crossed the road to look for a taxi, the nearby busker was singing Stairway to Heaven.
Steven's here! I wanted to stand and listen but a taxi with his 'For Hire' sign lit up, was coming towards me and my sensible head was saying put your hand out and stop it, which I did. I had to struggle to compose myself.

When I entered the hotel, I decided I so deserved a much better room and so I went up to Reception and complained that my room I had been allocated was no more than a cupboard with an en suite, on the 6th floor. At 10:30 p.m. I changed rooms, I was given a lovely double room on the first floor, that's more like it! I was very grateful.

Saturday 19th November

I got up very early and went downstairs to enjoy a full English breakfast and by 9 a.m. I was in a taxi, heading for the Royal College of Surgeons. I checked in, received a bag of goodies then went to find a seat and sit down. I was so looking forward to the Writers' Workshop.

I found the morning quite intense, it didn't help by the fact that I had a migraine. Michelle Pilley, Publishing Manager, spoke about writing a book, the publishing process, to self publish or get your book published. She talked about self publishing companies or traditional publishers and finally what did my head in 'Your Platform.' What is a platform? I thought it was that thing you stood on, to give a speech! I might add I was not alone!

Wow! That was a lot to take in. They certainly lost me a bit when they got to 'Your Platform.' Time for a much needed cuppa and two paracetamol.

Feeling a little better and ready for part two I sat down for the Q & A session before lunch. Then I went for a breath of fresh air and to try and find some lunch, which I found just around the corner on the High Street at PAUL'S. I enjoyed my lunch and was now ready for the afternoon session.

Julia Cameron, an American writer, who I was amazed to see shuffle out of her shoes and stand barefoot ready to commence speaking. She spoke on The Creative Writing Process. She had us interacting, it was enjoyable and very light hearted, with a few 'F' words dropped in here and there.

I have to say it shocked me, as in Weardale you don't normally hear a woman, especially a woman of a certain age, using the 'F' word.

She spoke for two hours, then we had a break before Dr. David R. Hamilton spoke. He was a handsome Billy

Connolly, well he sounded like him and he was an excellent speaker. He spoke for one and a quarter hours.

Afterwards the speakers signed their books at various stations in the hall. I decided to buy David Hamilton's Is Your Life Mapped Out because I believe it is and I also purchased How Your Mind Can Heal Your Body again it resonated with me.

Seven years ago, I was on twenty two tablets a day, told I had six blocked arteries and felt positively ill. I weaned myself off the tablets and as I walked each day I would say over and over

"My body is healthy, my arteries are flowing freely."

I have been off the tablets now for seven years and I feel the healthiest I have ever done.

Whilst waiting in the queue to get my books signed, I got talking to a lady called Banita, who asked if I would like to join her and her new friend for a meal. I said I would love to. Then I noticed a lady waiting to take a photo of David Hamilton, I asked her if she would like a photo of the two of them together and she said she would love to have one. Once the photo had been taken, I invited her to join us for a meal and she said she would love to join us.

As we were walking towards the door, taking our leave for the day, she turned to me and said "By the way, my name is Sara and I am from Dubai." To which I replied

"Hi, I am Pauline and I am going to Dubai on the 9th December."

(We exchanged phone numbers and have been in touch ever since, I have been over to Dubai four times and I have met up with Sara each time. Thank you Hay House for a beautiful friendship.)

On my way back to the hotel, after a very enjoyable meal, the taxi driver charged me half of what I had been charged that morning. When I said as much, he told me to go to Reception desk in the hotel and complain, as they had ordered the taxi for me.

Once he had dropped me off, I decided to go to Reception in the morning, as I would need another taxi. I went up to my room and enjoyed looking through my free gifts:- Conscious Writing by Julia McCutcheon, a Hay House Journal, 10 Secrets to Success, and Inner Peace by Dr. Wayne Dyer and lastly a Kindred Spirit Magazine.

I was in my element. I had had a truly excellent day. It had also been a long and tiring day mentally, so I decided I would have an early night. I was really looking forward to what tomorrow would bring.

Sunday 20th November

When Steven died I received the phone call at 3 a.m. in the morning. I now can't turn my mobile off at night just in case but if it does ring I feel physically sick, especially if it rings late.

So you can imagine how I felt when my room phone rang at 1:10 a.m. That feeling of panic! When I answered it, there was no-one on the other end of the phone.

The damage had been done, I was now wide awake. I picked up my mobile phone and went on to Facebook, the first thing that popped up was an exert from Children In Need, of parents who had lost both of their children.

I thought this is not happening to me! Paul and I are going to have great times together, he will always be there as I get older.

By now, I was so wide awake, I had to sit up and put the light on, my demons would not get the better of me. I put my faith in God and knew that all was well and my life and Paul's was good.

I started to think about the previous day and thought, yes I could do it. I could get my book published. I felt so inspired after the first day of the Writers' Workshop. I knew I had a lot of hard work ahead of me but I was sure that if I stayed focused and envisaged it happening and with a lot of commitment and God's guidance, I would get there.

I must stay focused about helping others through my writing. I was enjoying posting on Facebook, I liked to share my little adventures, hoping that it would inspire others to do so too.

I thought I might start to Blog about going through and coping with grief, I would have to see. The one thing I had to do was just stay confident and focused then I would be guided and given the help I needed, to do what I am meant to be doing and the reason why I have been put on this earth, my Divine pathway.

As I prepared for a new day, I hoped I could get back off to sleep or I would not be alert and take in what I needed to. I was hoping to get as much out of today as I had done yesterday. I was looking forward to meeting more beautiful people with whom I could connect with.

Well by 2:44 a.m. I felt I was surrounded by loving angels and I had nothing to fear, I was going to put my notebook and pen down, switch the light off and try and go back to sleep. I had almost written three A4 pages whilst sitting up in bed, just like Julia Cameron had suggested yesterday but maybe not at such an unearthly hour.

I had made a commitment with myself that I was going to start doing this every day when I got home and maybe when I go to Dubai I could go to a coffee shop there and write. It was no good going to No.10 at home because I would get too many interruptions.

I woke up feeling tired, when my alarm went off, not surprising really, after the night I had put in. It took me a while to get going but I wasn't in such a hurry today.

Breakfast was heaving when I got downstairs but it wasn't long before I was shown to a table and served. Afterwards I went to Reception and I explained to a very helpful French young gentleman, about how the taxi they had ordered for me yesterday, had charged me double the fare to what I had been charged last night on my return journey.

He asked if I would be needing a taxi again that morning and when I said I would and that I was actually going back to the Royal College of Surgeons, he told me to go to my room and get my case then by the time I returned, he would have a taxi waiting. He informed me that my journey would be free of charge.

252

I was learning, this weekend, not to just accept things as they are, but to speak up, I deserved better.

I got to the college and found a seat, today I was sitting in the front row, next to a lovely Indian lady and a lady called Debbie, who is a Medium but also deals with grief after loosing a pet.

The morning commenced, Michelle Pilley opened the morning session and talked about writing a proposal. It was hard for Michelle because she had to get the business side over to us and maybe that was why she picked first spot to catch us when we were as fresh as daisies.

Then Julia Cameron took the stage, she lightened the mood, she was brilliant and fun. We had a great session, singing, standing, shaking our arms in the air and doing 1-5's and what she called 'popcorn.' We stopped for a short break then Julia continued with a workshop until lunchtime.

Today there were seven of us that made our way to PAUL'S for lunch. It was good, we shared our thoughts about the morning session and how we were all eager to get back for the final session of the weekend.

The weekend was going by too quickly. Before I took my seat, I purchased another two books. I was going to be weighted down going home.

The afternoon session was more technical, Janey Lee Grace spoke on You Are The Brand (I bought her book How to be your own best P.R.) Then Kate Brookhurst spoke about how to build your own social media platform and to connect with your audience on line.

There was a comfort break before Michelle Pilley spoke on building your own website and brand. She also spoke about the competition the publishing company was running. There was a Q & As session before she closed the event.

I had no time to hang around. I found Sara, my new friend from Dubai, to say goodbye to and we agreed we would meet up when I go out to Dubai, in a couple of weeks.

Then I dashed off to catch my train and head for home, it had been a great weekend. Once I was on the train and settled in my seat, I offered up a prayer of grateful thanks to all of the speakers and organisers and everyone at the publishing company. It had truly been a brilliant weekend and I felt I had got some of my mojo back. I had found what I needed, a purpose to go forward.

Monday 21st November

I decided to start the way I meant to go on, as soon as I got up, I made a hot lemon and water and sat and wrote my Morning Pages. I found it amazing how I could just write three x A4 pages without thinking about what I was going to write about.

I had written about my mini adventure on Facebook and I sat and read the lovely encouraging comments people had posted. I was on a high. I had forgotten what it felt like.

I met one of the locals when I went for coffee, she was having problems with her teenager and was quite stressed out about it all. When I came home, I did a little research and I was able to obtain the information she so desperately needed. It was lashing down with rain by now but I had to get the information to her, so I wrapped up well and braved the storm.

She seemed really grateful that I would take time out of my day to help her. I couldn't do any other, my heart went out to her. I came home and listened to my affirmations CD, I am finding this recording very helpful. It was lifting my mood from negative to positive.

Tuesday 22nd November

This morning I woke up and reached out for my spectacles, which I put on my bedside cabinet every night, just before I go to sleep, but this morning I found that they were not there.

I looked around, on the floor, under the bed, inside my handbag, nothing! I decided to go and have my shower, as time was going by and I had little time to spare. I came back into the bedroom, once I was all done and opened my wardrobe doors to decide what I was going to wear. Then I heard a voice say, "Look behind the ashes."

I went and looked behind Steven's ashes and sure enough, there they were, my specs. I asked if Steven was playing silly beggars with me but I was thankful he had shown me where they were.

Once I had breakfasted, Alfie and I went to Sunderland for my twice weekly visit to the chiropractor. I had to weather the storm again to get there, as it still hadn't subsided, but I was looking forward to going down to the seafront once I had had my treatment.

I wasn't disappointed, the huge waves were crashing down onto the beach and flying high over the prom, absolutely fascinating to watch. The sea truly does fascinate me although I do have a fear of water, I love to be near the sea or on it in a boat/ship, although maybe not on a rough day like today.

I received a text to say the delivery of my Elton John concert tickets would be delivered today. I sent up a prayer to ask my angels to delay the delivery until I got back home.

I had literally just walked in the door and taken my wet coat off when the delivery guy knocked at my door. Thank you Angels, you are truly amazing!

Wednesday 23rd November

I was up at 6:10 a.m. my hot drink made, I settled down to do my Morning Pages. I felt so energised, once they were done. I like this, it is a great way to start the day and it puts me in the right frame of mind.

Thursday 24th November

Today I was going on a trip to Thursford, a very long journey lay ahead of me, which I was not looking forward to. It's not so much the journey as the number of times the coach has to stop. I know it is for the benefit of the driver, which I can understand but it just seems to take forever to get to where you are going.

At one of the coffee stops I learnt something from one of my dear friends, Pat. She told me, as we were sitting eating our complimentary mince pies, that during the Christmas period, one had to consume twelve mince pies, one for every month for the forthcoming year, to bring you luck and prosperity but you must not cut the mince pie with a knife, as this will stop the good luck coming to you, you are allowed to break it into pieces.

"Is this where I was going wrong?" I asked. "As I never eat twelve mince pies in December."

One thing is for sure I will try to eat twelve mince pies this year and hopefully I will have an excellent 2017.

Friday 26th November

We were visiting Peterborough Cathedral today. I had only set foot in the cathedral when I heard the organ start to play. The tears started to fall and just would not stop. I had to take myself outside and wait a half an hour until the rest of my party, who I was with, finished their tour. It was no good, I found it too upsetting. I couldn't understand it, because I had always gone to church but since Steven had died, after his funeral, I just couldn't manage to go to church.

On the evening, we visited the Thursford Christmas Spectacular which certainly was spectacular.

Much later on, when I was in bed, in the hotel, sleep just no where in sight, I let the tears fall. They had been hovering all night. Steven absolutely loved Christmas, his dream when he was young was to be Santa's helper.

Sunday 27th November

I had a text from Marion today, to say that she had copied all the CDs of Steven's music, ready for me to take to Dubai for Steven's friends. I went to collect them, I couldn't believe it, she had managed to put the picture of Steven with his Black Betty, on each and every one of them. I was so thrilled and grateful. They would love them, I just hope they have such a thing as a CD player to play them on.

Monday 29th November

I was feeling so energised and focused after doing my Morning Pages, Julia Cameron I will be forever in your debt for bringing them into my life. I don't know what it is about them but it really makes a difference to me.

I had to drive carefully today, the temperatures were below freezing and there was a thick white frost as far as the eye could see. I made my way to the undertakers, the memorial books were also ready for collection.

I had to go to the ex's to drop Steven's ashes off but he wasn't home and so I left them at my sister's house, who only lives on the next estate to him. She was delighted when I gave her the memorial book and CD but was tearful when I asked if I could leave Steven's ashes with her. I said he wanted to visit his Auntie Joy one last time. He used to love to go there when he was young.

Because I was feeling quite good today, I decided to go to Teeside to attend a meeting of the British Healers Association of which I am a qualified member of. They were so pleased to see me and I was so pleased I had made the effort to attend. It was a very productive meeting.

At my meditation group tonight, when I chose a card, I got the Christ consciousness. God was giving me the Bread of Life.

It had confirmed what I had been thinking, Steven has to work through me and that is why it was time for him to pass over. I feel him more and more each day.

Tuesday 30th November

Feeling quite ill today, feeling very sickly and not managing to eat much at all, a digestive biscuit and a toasted muffin. I had so much to do but it will all have to wait until another day.

DECEMBER

The huge lump in my throat is back! Could it be because I have to face a lot this month? I have what would have been Steven's 30th birthday, the internment of his ashes and Christmas, his much loved Christmas. A triple whammy!

First job - order the turkey and trimmings, then write the cards. The turkey was fine, the cards was a different matter. It was really difficult writing them. How do you wish people a "Happy Christmas" when you know that your Christmas will be the worst ever.

In fact I wished I could have hibernated for December and come out when the festivities were all over. I felt I was on automatic pilot, just going through the motions of what I was expected to do. A lot more tears and heartache. My heart does literally ache.

Thursday 1st December

I sat at my desk this morning and switched my MacBook on, only to find Steven's Harley Davidson pictures looking back at me. No way had I left my iPhoto open! I am amazed at how Steven can do this, he seems to get great pleasure in finding new ways of how to communicate with me. It truly does lift my heart when I notice these things. Steven's certainly here with me!

Friday 2nd December

I went with my local Women's Institute today to a Living North Christmas Fayre. In some ways I was dreading it, as everywhere I looked I was surrounded by Christmas.

My friends and I were sitting in the restaurant, at lunchtime, when something made me look over to my left. There, sitting just a couple of tables away, were three of Steven's teachers, his German and art teachers and his form teacher in his last year at school.

I went over to them to say hello and to ask if they were aware that Steven had died. They said they were and were deeply sorry to hear about Steven's death. More connections!

Tonight, as I sat and put all of my efforts into doing the scrapbooks for Ban and Paul, I thought if Paul doesn't know just how much his brother loved him then by the time he looks through his scrapbook, he would know beyond a shadow of a doubt. Every picture, Steven had his arm around his brother, he always protected him. Steven loved Paul so much, as I know Paul loved and still does love Steven.

I told Steven I was pregnant, on Christmas morning 1993. He climbed into my bed on the Boxing Day morning, put his arm around my neck and told me that finding out that he was going to get a baby brother / sister had been his bestest ever Christmas present!

Saturday 3rd December

It is thirteen years ago today since my brother Cecil died, it feels like a lifetime. I do miss my big brother, I always looked up to him.

I decided I would wrap my presents today. I was leaving home on 7th December and not returning until the 21st, ready for the internment of Steven's ashes on the 23rd. I needed to be organised!

I was supposed to be meeting my friend Jan, who was home for Christmas from Philadelphia, U.S.A. I rang her to say I was feeling very sickly, could we meet some other time, unfortunately her 92 year old dad answered the phone, Jan had popped out and so I left a message for her, with him.

A few minutes later the phone rang, it was Jan, she was worried as I never cancel. I just cried and cried. She told me that she would ring me later and check to make sure that I was okay.

Tonight I was supposed to be going to see Elton John with my friend Margaret. I had intended picking Margaret up in Sunderland before going for a meal in Newcastle and then we were going on to the concert.

I messaged Margaret to say I wasn't feeling very good, I felt very sickly and no way could I manage to go for a meal. I had also lost my mobile in the house which was doing my head in. She rang me back on my landline to say she would drive to Newcastle, once I had got to her home and not to worry, we wouldn't go for a meal.

I cried all of the way to Lynn's, Alfie's dog sitter. I was crying so much that Lynn asked me to stay there until I felt a bit better.

I did feel a little better by the time I got to Margaret's. I ate a crumpet, as she wouldn't let me go to the concert with nothing on my stomach.

Margaret drove and I have to say by the end of the evening I was pleased I had gone as I was feeling a little bit better.

Sunday 4th December

I had stayed at Margaret's overnight and because I was already at East Herrington, I decided to go and visit Jan, my sister Joy and Maria my old neighbour and lastly my friends from my old church, Gill and Roy to also deliver their Christmas cards at the same time. Yes, I was doing the rounds. I think I cried everywhere I went. I really felt I was loosing the plot.

Monday 5th December

Tonight Paul Skyped me to tell me that he wouldn't be in Dubai when I landed at 12:30 a.m. on Saturday. He would be away racing in Al Ain. He would leave the key to his apartment under the doormat outside his apartment. Brilliant!

I immediately went on to Facebook, when Paul had finished Skyping me and asked if any of my 'Dubai

Family' could pick me up and explained the reason why. Within minutes I had five offers. The first being Hassan, Steven's friend, President of the Warpigs. I was very grateful. Everything was going to be okay, I could sleep tonight.

Tuesday 6th December

Today I was meeting Jean, my friend who I had worked with when I worked for Midland Bank Ltd. We were meeting the girls we used to work with for a coffee then we were all going to the HSBC Pensioners Christmas Lunch, which was being held at the Old Assembly Rooms in Newcastle.

I felt very fragile by the time I got to Jean's, I wasn't sure if I was going to manage today.

I did okay though, I just felt as though I was in a bubble and everything was going on around me, I was just watching from a distance. I got through it and when it was all over, Jean and I went to look at Fenwick's Christmas windows, which we always do each year, then we did a little bit of Christmas shopping.

It was when we were in Eldon Square, that I heard a school singing carols and I had to say to Jean, I felt physically sick again. She took me into Boots and bought some Bach Remedy lozenges. I put one into my mouth and sucked on it. I have to say within minutes it seemed to do the trick. It seemed to take the edge off everything and my sickness subsided.

We got the bus back to Jean's, I had a cuppa and a slice of Stollen before I left to go to Trudy's for our meditation group's Christmas meditation. This was just what I needed.

Trudy had the room beautifully decorated, the table was set out with the spiritual cards for the evening, ready for each one of us to pick one at the end of the evening. Around the cards, there were candles and presents set out. It was truly a beautiful night.

The card I chose tonight was 'Let Go and Go With The Flow.' When I read the meaning, it was spot on, it meant a situation and that situation for me was Christmas and everything that came with it. So I decided there and then, that I would do precisely that, let go!

Wednesday 7th December

I made up my mind that I was going to Keswick today, it had been booked for months but what with how I had been feeling of late, I hadn't been sure whether I should go or not.

I worked methodically through the house, as you do when you go away. I can not go away unless I have cleaned the house from top to bottom. I also had to pack two cases. I was going straight to Newcastle Airport from Keswick, then flying to Dubai.

I wanted to be in Dubai for what would have been Steven's 30th birthday. Oh yes, I don't do things by half! I had always gone to Dubai for his birthday and I so wanted to be there this year. I needed to be with Paul and Steven's friends.

I checked and double checked that I had everything and eventually, all jobs done and satisfied I had everything I needed for the next fourteen days, I locked the door, got in my car and I got on my way.

The weather was wet and over the moors it was very misty, so I just took my time. I had nothing to hurry for, I stopped for a coffee and a scone on the way and eventually arrived and checked in at the Country Manor Hotel in Keswick for their 'Turkey and Tinsel' special.

Margaret had already checked in. She had sent me a text to say she was in the Skiddaw Hotel, in the centre of Keswick, drinking mulled wine with the rest of the crowd, if I wanted to join them.

I was tired, I had had a very busy day up until now and so I decided to just put my feet up and relax before I had to get ready to go down to dinner.

It was lovely meeting up with everyone later, catching up on each other's news. The meal was delicious and afterwards Margaret (a different one) and Stan, as per usual, had done a fun quiz for us all.

After a lot of fun and laughter we called it a day and retired to our rooms. I was feeling extremely tired.

Thursday 8th December

After a thoroughly enjoyable full English breakfast and a debate on who wanted to do what, I decided to have a day on my own. The others were going for a 'gin tasting' day. I hate gin and so it would have been the last thing on earth I would have wanted to do but everyone to their own, I say.

First I visited Thornthwaite Gallery, one of my favourites, I enjoyed a saunter around, looking at the beautiful pieces of art and craftwork on display which were for sale. I bought a couple of items then sat down and enjoyed a lovely cup of coffee, no scone, I was still full off my breakfast.

I sat and after some thought, decided I would go back into Keswick and wander around the town. I parked the car then went into the art gallery which was just beside the car park. It was lovely and they had some beautiful pieces on display. I bought a gift for my dear friend Sue, she is a homeopath and had been so kind, treating me over these past months, when my eczema had been horrendous. She had also given me some homeopathic treatments for grief, which I have to say had helped enormously, so I was buying her a token to show her my appreciation.

I also purchased a photograph frame with a dragonfly on the side of it, to put Steven's photo in and a lovely pair of turquoise earrings for myself. There's nothing like treating yourself!

When I went to the counter 'Sound of Silence' sung by Disturbed was playing. I explained to the lady that we had had this record played at Steven's funeral, she said she had goosebumps!

I said goodbye to her and went for a wander around the Market Place, not looking for anything in particular. I bought a few Christmas presents then I spotted a dragonfly pendant in a shop window, I just had to go into the shop to have a look at it.

I was a bit disappointed when the lady took it out of the window, it was smaller than what I had been looking for. She told me she had another, it had been hand crafted and when she brought it out, I just knew it was the one, my name was all over it. It had two green gems as it's body, (heart chakra, healing) and filigree wings made of silver. It was beautiful. When I mentioned the heart chakra, the lady connected with me immediately. I explained the reason why I wanted it and her eyes filled up. I was there for two hours talking to her.

Do you know the story of the dragonfly? Well the dragonfly lived in a pond with his friends and after a couple of years he noticed that his friends were leaving the pond and not returning. So after a while he decided to venture out to see where they had gone to. He realised once he had done so, that it was so beautiful on the other side that he had no desire to return.

It is a beautiful story and I feel it is quite appropriate to represent Steven and his passing. I see them everywhere I go, in all shapes and forms, they make me smile.

I bought the pendant and wear it on a long silver chain, close to my heart. It can also be used as a brooch. Beautiful!

I was now ready for a drink, so I crossed over to the other side of the street and sat in the conservatory of the

Skiddaw Hotel and enjoyed a toasted teacake and a cup of black coffee.

I sat there thinking about my day, about how successful it had been and how I had enjoyed talking to the lady in the art gallery and the lady in the little jewellery shop.

It was now time to return to the hotel. When I got back to my room, I packed what I could, then sat and watched some T.V., I had a leisurely bath and painted my nails. By which time Margaret had returned and we sat and chattered about our day until it was time to get dressed for the party night. We would be having a Christmas meal followed by a disco.

After the meal I started to feel very sickly again. Had I eaten too much? Or was it the thought of going to Dubai tomorrow? I also had to get myself to Newcastle Airport and the weather outside was atrocious, it was raining very heavily.

I got up for a few dances then said goodnight to everyone and took myself off to bed.

I had a very early start in the morning, no way did I want to miss my flight. I was also unsure of the roads as I had never driven that way to Newcastle before. I needed to be alert. I packed my clothes I had been wearing, checked in on line and had my boarding pass ready on my mobile phone. All sorted I went to bed for hopefully what would be, a good night's sleep.

Friday 9th December

I was up at 6:30 a.m. I quickly showered and got ready, said goodbye to Margaret then went downstairs where the night porter had a continental breakfast waiting for me. Tummy full and feeling more awake, I packed the car and set off on what would be a very long journey, I wouldn't be getting into Dubai until 12:30 a.m. tomorrow.

The rain was still very heavy and so with my Sat Nav on, (how grateful I am for my Sat Nav), I slowly pulled out of the car park, windscreen wipers working as fast as they could go, to try and clear the rain. I said farewell to Keswick for another year, all of my friends still tucked up in their beds, fast asleep, then I was on my way.

I have to say I was feeling a bit goggle eyed, my body does not like getting up at 6:30 a.m. but as I was later to realise, it was all well worth the effort. I drove out of Keswick onto the A69, heading north towards Carlisle before heading south to Newcastle.

I seemed to be ahead of the workers all of the way to Newcastle. It was very busy but all of the traffic was going in the opposite direction, thank goodness.

I arrived exactly one hour before I needed to, at 9 a.m. I had made really good time. Desperate for the loo, I decided to stop off at the local Dobbies Garden Centre, use their facilities then go and have a coffee in their coffee shop. The hour went by really quickly.

Coffee drunk, I went outside, it had stopped raining, enabling me to sort out my bags, putting some things

270

into the weekend case which I was leaving in the car and transferring some other items into my big case which I would need and which I was taking to Dubai.

All sorted I set off for the airport, which was just five minutes along the road.

I parked in the 'Meet and Greet' car park, checked in, unloaded what I was taking with me, locked the car and set off up the ramp towards the terminal.

As I walked in the door to the airport, I found I was right beside the Emirates check-in desks, which were just opening, brilliant timing.

All checked in, I made my way through security and duty free, bought a coffee and found a comfy seat beside the window enabling me to watch the planes arriving. I could feel the excitement building as I watched the Emirates plane come in to land. Not long now. I was amazed at how calm I was feeling, as I made my way to Gate 26.

My flight was called, each section announced, one at a time and told to board, but as I walked to the steps at the rear of the plane, I noticed the cargo being loaded on, that sick feeling came over me again. I was getting a flash back, thinking of Steven's coffin being loaded on to the plane, back in August. I felt really tearful and I tried hard to fight back the tears.

I was relieved that I was at the back of the plane and sitting in an aisle seat too. I had a female student sitting beside me, who was on her way to New Zealand to meet her mum and sister, who were already there. She was going to spend Christmas with them.

I enjoyed my meal and had settled down to watch some movies. I always class the Dubai flight as a three movie flight because you can just manage to fit in three movies from take off to landing in Dubai. It makes the flight so much shorter plus I can catch up on movies I have missed seeing at my local cinema.

I was okay until about an hour before we landed, the air hostess brought the ice creams around, then I got another flashback. It is strange how something so insignificant, can cause you to have such a big reaction. I was back in the galley, with the air hostess on that horrendous flight on the 6th August. It felt like it was years ago, since my beautiful and precious son had died.

Hassan and Yani, his wife, were waiting for me when I landed, I received a very warm welcome. They took me to Paul's apartment. I hadn't been to Dubai since Paul had moved, at the end of September from Jumeirah Village Two to Sport City.

Yani came in with me, to make sure I could get in and that all was well. We had a look around the apartment together, then opened the patio doors and walked out on to the balcony. Wow! What a fantastic view, you could see for miles, as Paul's apartment is on the twenty sixth floor. It was lovely seeing Dubai at night.

We talked for a while, she told me how Hassan was finding it hard to accept Steven's death, as were all the Warpigs. Then she had to go, as Hassan was waiting in the car outside.

I needed a cuppa before I went to bed, it had been one very long day. I would unpack in the morning.

Fortunately I had put my pj's and night bag on the top of my things in my case for easy access.

Saturday 10th December

Even though I had had such a late night, I still woke up at 7:30 a.m. I looked on Facebook and there I found lots of lovely well wishes from everyone. How did I manage without Facebook because wherever I am these days, I no longer feel alone.

Steven's friend, Danielle, had sent me a message to say, would I like to go out for the day, seen as Paul was racing in Al Ain? I quickly messaged her back to say I would love to go out. We arranged for her to pick me up at 1:00 p.m. I had nothing else planned for the morning and so I snuggled back down and had a couple more hours sleep.

Once up, showered, dressed and unpacked, Danni arrived. We decided to go to the Christmas Fayre.

We hadn't been there long, when the weather changed, big black clouds came over and the wind got up, just not what I expect when I am in Dubai, although it is their winter.

We decided to go to the Souk Madinat, my favourite mall. It is built like an ancient fort with lovely malls and the shops inside are quite different. Once you walk through the mall and out of the other side, there is a canal with boats sailing up and down, not dissimilar to Venice, but on a much smaller scale, with the Burj el Arab to the right, in the distance. We stopped for coffee and hot Cinnabons, a must if you are in Dubai, they are delicious and a very tasty treat. I first had them in America when I stayed with Jan, Steven used to love them.

We had had a Chinese sweet and sour with rice take away for lunch at the festival but that had been a few hours ago.

About 6:00 p.m. Danni dropped me off back at Paul's apartment. Tiredness came over me as I walked in to the apartment. I lay down on the settee and slept until Paul returned, a few hours later.

At 9:30 p.m. we walked over to the Sports Complex, which was not too far away. I was elated, it was so good to see him, I had missed him so much. We had a hot snack then walked back and off to bed, both of us shattered.

Sunday 11th December

Today would have been Steven's 30th birthday, Paul had the day off work and at first he said did I fancy going to the beach?

I was feeling quite tearful and just wasn't sure what I wanted to do, unknowingly the Universe had a very memorable day in store for the two of us.

Suddenly Paul changed his mind and suggested that we go to Abu Dhabi, because although he races there, he had never visited the Sheikh Zayed Grand Mosque nor the Emirates Palace Hotel and so I thought it was a great idea.

I had had a wonderful day just Steven and I, when I had visited Steven in Dubai, after my mum, Steven's beloved Nana, had died. Paul was still in the U.K. at that time and Steven because he had just gone there in the January, wasn't allowed any time off work to come home for her funeral.

That day we had visited the mosque and the Emirates Palace Hotel, Steven had loved it and I have to admit, so had I.

Paul and I breakfasted at Natalie's cafe, I enjoyed poached eggs on a muffin washed down with a black coffee and whilst we were having breakfast I told Paul about what the Medium, had told me about when I see a Dragonfly, it is Steven telling me he is there. I was also wearing my Dragonfly necklace which I had purchased in Keswick.

As we walked out of the cafe, Paul said "Mam there's a dragonfly!" Neither one of us had ever seen a dragonfly in Dubai before. Confirmation, I would say!

We set off for Abu Dhabi, our first stop being the huge mosque, it is so impressive, as you approach it, this huge whiter than white building. We parked up, went our separate ways as I had to queue for an abaya.

Whilst in the queue I noticed a large sign saying that you had to hand in your passport when you borrowed the abaya. I didn't have mine with me! Oh no! I had changed handbags that morning and had decided I wouldn't need my passport and so I had left it behind in Paul's apartment. I hadn't needed it the last time I was here.

To pass the time away, whilst I had been waiting in the queue, I had been talking to a lovely muslim lady from Seattle, U.S.A. I had already told her the reason for Paul and I visiting that day. When I explained my plight, she told me not to worry, if I let her stand in front of me, she would get mine on her passport, as you were allowed to borrow two abayas on one passport.

I was so grateful. She got our abayas and we left the cloakroom and put them on. Paul was waiting for me outside. The lady told me that we must take our time, she understood just how special our day was and she would meet us where we had to leave our shoes.

Well we went our own way, the lady with her husband and little boy and myself with Paul but then I suddenly realised that we were all dressed the same, it was like a Carry On movie, how was I going to recognise her?

We decided that her shoes were near to where we had put our shoes, so if when we were finished looking around and taking many photos of the mosque, we would go and sit near to the shoe racks where hopefully she would find us. She would not be given her passport without my abaya.

The mosque holds 7,000 worshippers. The exquisite crystal chandeliers, which may I add have a ladder inside of them for cleaning purposes, match the stained glass windows and the flowers engrained in the marble going along the marble floor and up the pillars were also represented in the pattern of the carpet. I have never seen anything so beautiful in my life. It truly is exquisite.

Unfortunately we weren't able to see all of what Steven and I had seen three years ago, as they now had certain areas roped off but Paul could still see the majority of the mosque. We both enjoyed our visit. We met up with the lady from Seattle, I went with her to return the abayas, thanked her so much for her thoughtfulness and kindness, before Paul and I set off for our next stop, the Emirates Palace Hotel.

Again this was so much busier than my previous visit and it looked as though there was a wedding party arriving for their wedding reception. Here, everywhere the eye can see, is gold, the furnishings, the carpet, the marble flooring, the lights, literally everything, it's amazing. There is even a vending machine where you can purchase a gold ingot or gold jewellery. We had an added bonus because everywhere we looked today, there were the most beautiful Christmas decorations on display.

We went in search of a table but they were all taken. I asked the head waiter if he could find us a table for two. He asked if we minded sitting at the bar and I said certainly not, as long as we could get seated. I just wanted Paul to enjoy the experience.

The gentleman wandered off and asked the ladies sitting around the bar, to remove their handbags and shopping from the seats enabling him to rearrange the
seating to enable Paul and I to sit together at the end of the bar.

Well we mustn't have been sitting at the bar for more than a couple of minutes when he returned and asked us to follow him, he had found us a lovely table for two. I was absolutely delighted. So off we went, following the gentleman as he showed us to our table.

I ordered non alcoholic cocktails for the two of us, because today was a National Holiday to commemorate a prophet's festival, no alcohol could be consumed from 7 p.m. the night before until 7 p.m. that night but it didn't matter because we were just determined to make the best of the situation.

We looked at the menus and decided we would have camel burgers and chips. The burgers came, beautifully presented, with edible 24crt gold flakes on them. So unreal but there again this was Abu Dhabi and anything was possible. Paul, like Steven three years previously, just had to take the opportunity to take a photo and put it on Facebook.

Once the drinks arrived we drank a toast to Steven, wishing him a happy 30th Birthday. It was truly special and for Paul to experience what Steven and I had, made it so much more special.

We sat and thoroughly enjoyed our meal and cocktails and once we had finished we decided we had better start making our way home, as time was not on our side.

We arrived back at Paul's apartment, we had a quick shower and changed. Danielle came and picked us up at 7 p.m. and we made our way to the Irish Village where hopefully his Warpigs and Black Eagles friends were going to join us for a birthday celebration. Some of Paul's friends were also coming.

We were sitting enjoying our drink, when Danielle said she could hear bikes. I listened but couldn't hear anything then I heard the roar, all of his friends and partners had been on a bike ride in Steven's memory before they had come to join us. There were thirty two of us in total, Steven would have been delighted. His friends had turned out in force with their girlfriends and wives.

All night I was waiting for a sign to let us know Steven was with us.

We had a wonderful night and just before we left, we had to have a group photo taken. It was whilst we were all standing together that I heard it. I could hear the group playing Nickleback's song 'This is how you remind me of what I really am.'

This was the confirmation I had been waiting all night for. I just knew Steven would let me know he was here and I looked at Yani who smiled and agreed with me, Steven was indeed letting us know he was with us. Again it was a memorable song, one Steven used to play when learning to play the guitar.

Paul and I returned to his apartment happy, it had been one very special, memorable day. Thank you Lord. I just knew I had to be here amongst the people Steven loved so much.

Monday 12th December

Today Paul was off to work and I had arranged to meet up with Sara, who I had met at the Writers' Workshop. Sara picked me up at 1 p.m. and took me for a most enjoyable lunch at the Emirates Golf Club. We spent five wonderfully, enjoyable hours together. We ate a most delicious lunch of Beef Thai salad followed by Lasagne, and finished off with a fruit platter and coffee.

I couldn't eat all of my lasagne, so I actually asked for a goodie bag and took it home with me for Paul's supper, which I have to say he really appreciated and enjoyed, when he got in from work. The portions in Dubai are so big.

Tonight Paul took me to the Karama. This is quite a seedy place, lots of shops, in the old part of Dubai, selling look a likes and may I add they are not cheap! I bought a couple of items, I felt obliged to after Paul had taken the trouble to take me.. All done we went back to the apartment and went straight to bed, exhausted.

Tuesday 13th December

A free day all to myself today, so what do I do when I am on my own? I give myself a treat! I take myself off to a book shop but not just any bookshop, no. I was going to go to my favourite bookshop, Kinokumiya in the Dubai Mall.

If you are ever in Dubai and love books then this is the book shop for you, it is so worth a visit. Mind you take plenty of money with you, as if you are like me, I always come away with an armful of books.

After about two hours I had decided which books I wanted to purchase. My best find was Julia Cameron's trilogy in hardback. The Complete Artist's Way, Walking in this World and Finding Water. I was so excited, you would have thought I had found a pot of gold on the bookshelf. I have to say there was only one copy and it had my name on it.

When I later phoned Sara to tell her, she was amazed, as the last time she was in that book store, she wasn't able to find any of Julia Cameron's books, I'm even more certain it was waiting for me. I really couldn't believe my eyes. Was this a gift from God or what?

By the time I went and paid for my haul, it was time for lunch and a coffee as it was getting on to 3 p.m. Not far away along the Mall, I found a comfy seat in a coffee shop and ordered lunch, chicken caesar salad with a mint lemonade, delicious. I sat and wrote for an hour, I was in my element.

I then ordered two pistachio macaroons and a cup of black coffee. I hadn't a care in the world and I only had me to please. I so appreciate quality time on my own, 'Me Time!'

On my way back to the taxi rank I spied some black/gold and some silver sandals which were just what I had been looking for, as I was going on a Caribbean cruise in January, with some friends. Yes, they had my size and yes they fit, brilliant, so I bought both pairs.

Time to go to the taxi rank now, my bags were heavy and no way could I have bought another item, my arms were aching as it was but what a fabulous day I had had.

Once I got to the taxi rank, I was asked if I would like an Imperial taxi. I certainly did not! The one and only time I had gotten into one, he drove off then told me it would cost two hundred Dirhams. I made the driver take me back to where he had picked me up.

Using the normal yellow cabs, my journey had cost me forty seven Dirhams, on the way to the Dubai Mall, quite a substantial difference. Paul keeps telling me, you have to show them who is boss! Well I had certainly done that.

It must have been about 5 p.m. when I got back to Paul's apartment. I lay down and had an hour's sleep because at 6:15 p.m. I had to get showered, changed and be down at Apartment 1007 for 7:00 p.m. Paul's friend Emily was taking me to the Mall of the Emirates to see the Christmas decorations and to have a girly night, whilst Paul was working late.

The decorations were spectacular, there were dancers dressed like fairies, who were dancing to music around the Christmas tree, another huge tree was made of Ferrera Roche, amazing! It was all very impressive and I did notice that most of the shops had winter stock in, just like in the U.K. The Emirates think it is winter, whilst I think a very comfortable twenty seven degrees is summer. So I am dressed in sundresses whilst they are wearing jumpers, jackets and even fur coats.

We ate at the Cheesecake Factory, one of my favourites, before calling it a day. I had had a very full day. It is amazing just what you can pack into a day in Dubai plus the Malls are open until midnight. Very long days!

You must think I am always eating out in Dubai but that's what you tend to find. Very rare do we eat in and if we do, then it's quite possible we would order a takeaway from the local restaurant. You can get anything delivered, free of charge from a Subway sandwich to your Christmas dinner pre-cooked with all the trimmings. You can even phone your local supermarket and they will deliver anything, to your door, it doesn't matter how small, there won't be any charge.

Yes it is another world, a much different world but I have to say I love it and the people there, they are so friendly. It is a very special country.

Well I got home, Paul was already in bed, he had had a long day. So I went straight to bed, not that I could sleep. I tossed and turned until I dropped off to sleep, then I had a nightmare. I was dreaming about Steven's bones, which were in a bag, shrinking to nothing.

What a night! I must have eventually dropped off to sleep around 6 a.m. and I slept until 11 a.m.

Wednesday 14th December

I woke feeling very subdued today. I suppose considering the night I had had, it was not surprising. I wasn't sure what to do today, as Paul was again at work all day. Then my mobile phone pinged.

It was one of Steven's friends, Jane, asking me out for lunch. Oh how lovely! I quickly got out of bed, ironed Paul's washing and washed down the kitchen benches.

I have to earn my keep some how! To be honest, I love doing it, I feel as if I have got my old job back, being mam, it's amazing how I miss it when I go back home.

Once the jobs were done, I showered, dressed and was ready for Jane picking me up at 1:30 p.m. We headed off to Motor City, just beside the Go-Kart track, where

Paul is based, if the team is not racing. We ate at the Crumbs Elysee.

The food was both tasty and healthy. The conversation flowed, so much so, it was 6 p.m. by the time we left the restaurant. They certainly do not hurry you out of restaurants in Dubai.

When I returned to the apartment Paul had already rung me, to say we were being picked up at 8 p.m. tonight, we were going out with nine of his friends to Apres, for a Christmas meal.

I love this restaurant, as it has huge windows overlooking the ski slopes in the winter village. I love watching everyone having fun in the snow, wearing their snowsuits and skiing. It is so hard to believe you can have this experience in Dubai, when it is so hot outside.

I enjoyed both the company and my meal of salmon, leek and pasta. I felt like a mother hen with her brood. At 11 p.m. we all said farewell, wished everyone a Happy Christmas and headed for home. Another fantastic day filled with fun and friendship.

Thursday 15th December

I had had another dreadful disturbed night. It took me all morning to pull myself together. I wrote, read, went on Facebook and eventually at 1 p.m. I dragged myself into the shower, then got dressed.

I was in a quandary of what I should do and in the end I decided I would go to JBR beach. I went off in search of a taxi. You rarely walk anywhere in Dubai, normally because it is too hot and dusty.

I was lucky, I had only reached the corner of the street when one arrived. It didn't take long, he was a chatty Indian driver. He told me he worked in Dubai for eight months of the year then he returned to India for the other four months, to spend time with his family. He sent most of his money back to his family in India, enabling his two daughters to have private education but whilst he was in Dubai, he would Skype them every day to talk to them.

When we got to my destination and he pulled up by the roadside, it looked unfamiliar. So much had changed since I was there last December. So many new buildings had been erected. There were a lot more hotels, shops, beautiful paintings of horses and sea life.

I noticed an exquisite Italian hotel, La Bohem, which reminded me of my holidays in Barga, Tuscany and the opera, which I had seen in the medieval opera house there. Such happy memories.

I walked along the sea front getting familiarised with my surroundings. I noticed there was even a gym and a children's play area situated on the beach. The latter being under cover, to protect the children from the sun. There was also lots of market stalls and a children's fairground, I must say the latter I felt was a bit tacky and lowered the tone somewhat. It was stuck in-between some beautiful water features and rather expensive shops.

About 3 p.m. this seems to be my normal lunchtime these days, I found a PAUL'S coffee shop and sat at one of the tables outside and ordered my lunch. I thought I would keep it healthy and so ordered a prawn and avocado salad sandwich with a refreshing crushed mint lemonade.

I struggled to eat all of the sandwich but what I had, was very tasty. I paid the bill then wandered back along the sea front. I had seen two long sundresses which would be ideal for the cruise and so I decided to go back, try them on and buy them if they fit, which they did.

Fed, watered and a little bit retail therapy done, it was now time for a little exercise. I took my sandals off and walked in the sea, right along the shoreline. The water was lovely and warm but cool enough to ease my aching, hot feet. When I got quite a long way along, I turned and walked all the way back.

The sun was starting to set, the birds were enjoying a paddle and people were starting to pack up and make their way home or back to their hotels.

I found a seat, just on the walkway, above the sand and sat for a while, people watching and watching the dynamics between families. By now the beach was almost clear and I thought it was time to head back to the apartment.

It must have been about 6 p.m. when I returned, siesta time! When I woke up I read until Paul came home from work at 8:45 p.m. It had been a very long day for him, he had been up and out since 5:30 a.m.

Once showered and changed we went for a Sunday Roast, well Paul did, I just had a children's portion of fresh fish and chips, it was just like what we have in England.

As soon as we had eaten, we went home to bed. In the morning, Paul had asked if I would like to go with him to work. I jumped at the chance, I would love to go.

He was working at Yas Marina F1 Race Track in Abu Dhabi, Sean Babbington, who was driving for Energy Racing Dubai, and who is also a very good friend of Paul's, was competing in the F4 race there. Sean was World Champion in Karting and had moved on to race F4 cars.

Friday 16th December

The alarm went off at 5:30 a.m. I was up, showered and dressed before Paul got up on the third alarm call. We were all set to go by 6:25 a.m. Sean was meeting us in the parking lot, he also lived in the same apartment building. He appeared with his pillow tucked under his arm. He planned to curl up on the back seat of Paul's car and sleep all the way to Abu Dhabi.

I was just going to sit and enjoy watching the dawn break and the beautiful sun rise. When it did, the moon was still high in the sky. This was so well worth getting up at such a God forsaken hour for.

Breakfast was a quick stop off at McDonalds on the way. I was feeling quite excited, as we pulled in to the car park of the Formula One Racing Circuit. We made our way to the pits.

At 8:35 a.m. Paul and I made our way to the other side of the track, to time Sean, as he went out for his first practice lap. On the way, we met one of Paul's old lecturers from Gateshead College, where Paul had studied Motor Racing after he had been 4th in the British Go Karting Championships and had also spent a day with Lewis Hamilton. It was part of the prize of coming fourth.

This lecturer had apparently met me when I was seventeen, when he was visiting Sunderland and District Motor Club of which I was a member of. I certainly couldn't remember him. What a small world! He was actually there doing the commentary for the endurance race, which was going on in-between the Formula 4 races.

Paul and I got to where we needed to be and of course, we had to take a few photos, that is in-between watching and timing Sean. Today, Energy Racing Dubai team had hired an engineer, who just happened to have worked for Michael Schumacher. He had been hired to help Energy Racing Dubai, as they were just venturing into Formula 4.

When we went back to the pits this guy was sitting whistling 'The Sound of Silence.' I called Paul and Sean over to listen, we had just been talking about all of the different things that had happened since Steven had died. We all smiled at each other, it would be a good day, Steven was watching over us.

After two practice rounds, we went into the hospitality lounge and had lunch. It was then time for Sean's first race. He came 4th. I had felt sick watching him, I had prayed he would stay safe and not crash. Prayers were indeed answered.

I felt sorry for Sean, because when he came back into the Pits, the mechanics and Paul were all onto him, telling him what he should or shouldn't have done. I could tell he was upset.

Peter, the engineer, talked through the race with Sean. It hadn't helped that just before Sean had gone onto the track to get ready for the race, the electrics had fused in the pit and they had to frantically manually wind up the electronic door, separating the pit from the track. It had been manic!

Sean's next race saw him finishing third, winning him a podium finish. Well done Sean, I was so pleased for him. Eventually at 7:30 p.m. we got into the car and left the track. Time to go home. It had been one very long but very enjoyable and memorable day.

Paul is the team manager for Energy Racing Dubai and I had thoroughly enjoyed watching him at work, in fact I was really proud of him and very impressed. I had sat and watched as Paul went through the races with Sean, Sean had the video of the race on his laptop and Paul on his laptop had the statistics. Paul sat going through every inch of the track with Sean informing him as to where and when Sean should break and accelerate to enable him to achieve better results.

Burger King was our supper stop on the way home and yes, it was straight to bed when we got in. Paul had to be up again in the morning at 5 a.m. but Mam, she was staying in bed.

Saturday 17th December

Today, Tracey, one of the Go Karting mums messaged me to say she would pick me up at 11 a.m. and take me out for the day.

We decided to go to the Miracle Garden. It certainly is a Miracle Garden. How they can get the flowers to grow there in the desert, in such extreme temperatures, is amazing. The gardens were striking, every which way you turned there was exquisite beauty. There was even an Emirates plane made out of flowers.

Afterwards Tracey took me to the Crumbs Elysee Cafe for lunch and I enjoyed an omelette today. We sat for a couple of hours chatting, you would have thought we had been friends for years.

I had only met Tracey and Jane at Steven's memorial service so I feel very grateful that I have been given the opportunity to get to know them better and to form friendships.

Tracey, in the past, had often invited Paul for his Sunday dinner, whereas Jane used to go riding with Steven on their Harley Davidsons.

At 4:30 p.m. Tracey dropped me off at Paul's apartment and I let myself in, sat down and read until Paul arrived back from work.

Saturday 18th December

Paul was up and out very early this morning to go to work. I decided when I woke up I would do the washing and ironing and clean the apartment.

All done and dusted, I took myself off up to the 34th floor, the sun terrace and pool. I found a sun bed in the shade alongside the outside pool and lay down. I was going to have a couple of hours reading or until such a time that the heat became unbearable.

I lasted about two hours before I was forced by the heat, to go in search of some air con and a cold drink. The washing had dried out on the balcony, so I spent the next hour or so ironing the clothes.

When Paul arrived home from work, we went back to the pool. It was a bit cooler by then and much more pleasant. It was lovely just lying relaxing and so we stayed there until the sun went down.

Tonight, Paul and I along with Sean and Ritchie, (he also worked for Energy Racing Dubai) had been invited to Kevin and Sara's (Paul's boss and his wife) for Sunday roast.

When we got there and whilst we were waiting for dinner to be served, the guys had a water fight with the kids. Kev, Sara and I sat and had a drink before sitting down to our meal. It was a really pleasant night and I have to say the meal was absolutely delicious. 10 p.m. time to head off home to bed.

Monday 19th December

Paul had a meeting early this morning and because I was feeling really tired, I decided to stay in bed and have a lie in.

It must have been around noon when Paul returned and we decided to go off to Nasimi Beach, which has Atlantis as a backdrop. It was beautiful, there were very comfy sun lounges, waiter service to the sun lounges and the sea was just a few feet away, perfect!

I am so lucky to have these opportunities, I suppose it is a little consolation for having my son work 3,000 miles away from home.

As the sun was setting, we made our way home, for a shower and a change of clothing. Tonight we were hitting the Dubai Mall.

Boy, does my boy like to browse. By the time we were ready for home I had a blister about two inches in diameter on my right heel, my groin and hip were causing me jip and my feet were throbbing. I am so not used to walking for four hours round a Mall and what do you know? He came back and ordered what he wanted, on line! I fell exhausted into my bed!

Tuesday 20th December

My last day in the U.A.E. I was feeling quite low at the thought of going back to the U.K. It took me a while to get going this morning, I was all aches and pains after our shopping trip last night.

I spent the morning sorting out everything and packing my case. Paul arrived home about 5 p.m. and we went to pick up his shirts, which he had been having made for him. We had a quick meal on the way home, finished our packing and were in bed by 10 p.m. We had to be up by 4 a.m. for our Emirates flight back to the U.K. Yes, Paul was coming home with me for the internment of Steven's ashes and of course Christmas.

Wednesday 21st December

The taxi picked us up at 4:45 a.m. to take us to the airport. Even at this unearthly hour the roads were not quiet. We didn't seem to be at the airport long, once we had checked in, gone through security and duty free, before our flight was being called.

Paul and I had two aisle seats opposite each other. Mine was on the edge of the four in the middle of the plane and a family were taking up the rest of the seats, with the mum sitting behind me. Paul had a spare seat to his left and so I asked the family if they would like my seat, which they willingly accepted.

Later in the flight I was so grateful I had changed seats because the little boy who would have been sat next to me, was a bit of a tinker and I don't think I would have had any peace.

I couldn't settle to watch a film, I kept nodding off to sleep. The flight made good time and we landed in Newcastle thirty minutes sooner than what was expected.

I was so pleased I had my car parked in the 'Meet and Greet' as we were loaded up and away in no time at all. I dropped Paul off at his dad's house then I went to see Steven's gravestone. It had been laid in preparation of the internment on Friday.

I stopped off at the Arnison Shopping Centre on my way home, to get my Christmas food shopping. I was just about at the checkout in M & S food department, when I got a very disgruntled phone call from Paul. He had taken my case by mistake, we both have the same cases.

I suggested I wait for him where I was, so that we could swap our cases. This would save him coming all the way to Wolsingham. I have to say he was certainly in a strop when he arrived, he was meeting his new girlfriend for a late lunch. Oh well everything is as it should be, so they say.

I went off to collect Alfie from the dog sitter. It was 5:30 p.m. by the time I made it back home. The plane had landed at 12:15 p.m.

By the time I had put the shopping away, I was absolutely shattered. The cases would have to wait for another day to be unpacked.

I made a cuppa and sat down to open my post. I was delighted to find I had won three twenty five pound cheques from the Premium Bonds. An early Christmas present, thank you very much. Then an early night was a must.

Tuesday 22nd December

What a busy day I had in store. I got up early and unpacked both cases, yes I also had the one from my visit to the Lake District and my hand luggage.

Next job, was going to Sunderland for my chiropractor appointment but on the way I picked up the DVDs I had had done at the Tesco superstore in Durham.

Once I had had my treatment I took Alfie for a walk along the seafront but we couldn't dawdle today, I had a guy coming to fit two new blinds at 1:30 p.m. I literally just made it in time, as he had just pulled up at my door when I got back home.

Blinds all fitted, it was time to do the washing and go and get the rest of the food I needed for over the Christmas period, from the local shops on the High Street.

It must have been about 7 p.m. when I could say that all the jobs were done and I was able to make my meal then sit down in front of the T.V. until bedtime.

Friday 23rd December

I woke up, with what felt like a huge black cloud, hanging over me. I got up, made myself a hot drink, then went and switched the T.V. on. I needed to see what the weather forecast was for the day. Storm Connor was forecast to hit the North East that day with 80mph gusts of wind. It was forecast to hit at the exact time we were having the internment of Steven's ashes.

I went upstairs and prayed. The tears were coming thick and fast. I left home about 9:45 a.m. and cried all the way to Sunderland. I was going to my friend Jan's, whose nephew's wife Sarah had done a wreath for us and then Jan and Jeff were coming with me to the church for the short service. They had been in the U.S.A. when we had had Steven's funeral. Jan and Jeff had known Steven for all of his short life.

By the time I got to Jan's I was hysterical. I wasn't sure if I would be able to go through with it. Jan made me a drink and I wrote the card to go on the wreath before we set off to go to the church, where the service was being held. When we arrived the priest, several members of my family along with Paul and his dad were waiting for us to arrive.

The priest said prayers inside of the church, then we had to brave the storm, as we stepped outside of the church. The priest had taken me to one side before the short service to suggest that maybe, due to the weather conditions, only he should scatter the ashes into the grave. I had totally agreed with him. With the gusts of wind being so strong, it was possible Steven's ashes would end up scattered all over the graveyard. Steven would have had the last laugh if that had happened.

We all gathered around the grave and the priest bent right down. I was fearful he would end up falling into the grave, he had had to stoop so low but everything considered, he managed brilliantly. He asked if we would all like to go and wait inside of the church whilst the gravedigger filled in the grave and placed the gravestone on top.

Would I have ever dreamed that when I placed Steven into his cradle when he was born, that one day I would be standing, watching, as his ashes were being scattered into the cold, sodden earth.

When the gravestone was in place, we were asked if we would like to go back outside to see it. Jeff handed me the wreath. Well I hadn't been outside more than a few seconds when the wind caught the wreath and whipped several of the flowers out. Someone quickly picked them up off the ground before they were blown away. Everyone agreed that I should take the wreath home and keep it there until such a time when the storm had subsided, then I could bring it back and place it on Steven's grave. The card had blown off the wreath. His dad had picked it up and put it in his pocket. He never returned it.

Everyone except Jan and Jeff went to the local pub to get warm afterwards. There was a roaring fire waiting to greet us. We got a drink, then sat and chattered but at 1 p.m. I said my farewells, wished everyone a Merry Christmas then I headed for home. The storm was due to peak at 3 p.m. and I didn't want to be stranded.

Later that day I had afternoon tea with three of my friends, Anne, Marion and Jeanette at Stanhope Old Hall. It was cosy, with another roaring fire and a beautiful Christmas tree, all lit up. The perfect picture. We always try to have some quality time together over the Christmas period plus we had our presents to exchange and it was good to end the day on a positive note.

Afterwards I went home to finish off wrapping the rest of my Christmas presents and pay my bills then time for a treat, I sat and watched the Strictly Come Dancing final, which I had recorded whilst I was away in Dubai.

I had got through it all, how, I do not know but I had managed. Life truly does go on.

Saturday 24th December

By 8:15 a.m. I was up and organised, having already collected my pre-ordered turkey and bread. 9:30 a.m. the reader from church came and gave me Holy Communion, as I still felt I couldn't go to the normal service in church.

I spent most of the day delivering presents. Paul and I went to my sister's for tea before going to the local carol service. I was pleased we were tucked in to the corner seats at the back of the church.

We ended up at Jan's for her annual Christmas party. Paul only staying for an hour, before he was off to Chester-le-Street to meet up with friends, having promised faithfully he would be home for Christmas morning.

I found it very hard at the party, everyone was jolly but I just didn't feel like celebrating. I stayed in the kitchen and spoke to people as they came through to help themselves to some supper, but by 9:15 p.m. I was ready to go home.

I felt relieved to be back home, I opened my front door, took my mask off, so to speak, relaxed and allowed myself to feel how I was truly feeling, so bereft. I took my coat off, sat down and watched T.V. I must have fallen asleep, as I woke up at 1:30 a.m. and took myself off to bed.

Sunday 25th December

Our first Christmas without Steven, my heart was breaking. Steven had been what Christmas was all about. He would get so excited, so much so, he could never get to sleep and would be up by 4 a.m. ready for all of us to go downstairs, to see if Santa had been and to open our presents.

Even Paul had said, how were we going to cope, as Steven had always been the one to get us motivated. There was a huge hole in our lives, which would never be filled.

I got up and quietly opened Paul's bedroom door, yes he had got home safely. Thank you Lord.

I went and had a shower then sat and cried. Paul came in and suggested that we should go downstairs and see if Santa had been.

So the two of us went downstairs together to open our presents, even though it was the last thing we, if we were perfectly honest, wanted to do. We were just going through the motions.

When Paul opened up his scrapbook which I had made for him, he started to cry, which made me cry again. He came over to where I was sitting and we just hugged each other, tears streaming down our faces, we knew the pain the other was going through. It was so, so hard. Nothing prepares you for this.

When the tears eventually subsided, we finished opening our presents before we had our breakfast then I took Alfie for his morning walk and Paul went back to bed to get some much needed sleep.

I prepared the dinner and when Paul was up and dressed we walked to our local pub, The Black Lion, where we had arranged to meet Marion and Wayne. We only had one drink with them but it was good to get out. We wished them a Merry Christmas and then went back to our respective homes, dinner was waiting to be finished off, then enjoyed.

I don't know how but I think I must have had Divine assistance, as every now and again I was keep getting a prompting from this voice in my head, to put the sausages in, make the stuffing, put the potatoes in to roast. I was on automatic pilot but I have to say our dinner was the best ever, even Paul said so too.

If I am honest, I felt spaced out the whole time I was preparing and cooking the lunch. In fact the whole week leading up to Christmas I had felt I was in a bubble, watching people celebrate but not being a part of it.

After dinner, Paul and I went to sit down in the lounge to watch T.V. but we both fell asleep. We slept all afternoon and only woke up when it was time for Paul to go to his dad's.

I walked Alfie, made myself a turkey sandwich and sat down to watch Strictly but again I fell asleep and ended up watching it on catch up. I made myself have an early night, I was exhausted both mentally and physically.

Monday 26th December

I decided to take Alfie to Seaburn today, it was a beautiful but very cold morning, ideal for a brisk walk along the seafront and get the cobwebs blown off us.

I parked up, we must have been about half a mile from the sea front, then briskly walked down to where the Boxing Day Dip was being held. The first group were just coming out of the water when we got there, they must have been freezing. There were hundreds of people both competing and spectating, I didn't envy them one bit. Mind you, they all looked as though they were having great fun.

Steven and Paul had both done the Boxing Day Dip, when we had had the hotel, they had joined in with our staff. I can remember them saying that the worst part was when the firemen hosed them down with the hose pipe before they ventured into the sea.

I didn't stay long as the wind was biting cold. Alfie and I walked back to the car and headed for home, I was thinking of my tasty turkey and stuffing sandwich waiting for me when I got back home.

Today was a day for relaxing and so once I had had my lunch, I sat and did my knitting in front of the T.V. Paul came to see me but ended up asleep most of the time. This seems to be the norm when he comes here. He sits down, relaxes and before you know it, he's asleep.

My motto this year is 'Let go and let God.' I am accepting and being grateful for everything. I feel so peaceful and I was enjoying my day, even though my heart was aching and I was missing Steven so much. I kept thinking he wouldn't want me sitting crying all the time.

Tuesday 27th December

I felt exhausted again today, is it the grief that makes me feel so tired? Maybe that is the same for Paul too. I gave myself permission to have a lie in and got up at 11 a.m. Once I was up and dressed I took Alfie for a lovely long walk along the riverside, then when I returned home, I sat and meditated. It seemed like ages since I had done so.

I felt a lot better afterwards, so much so, I spent the afternoon making asparagus soup and iced turkey curry. Paul and his new girlfriend were coming for tea and staying over.

Wednesday 28th December

When I checked my emails this morning, I had had an email from the Medium, she was doing a spiritual workshop, 4th and 5th February and I decided I was going to put my name down for it. I felt drawn to do it.

Paul went off to play golf with his cousin Matthew, dropping his girlfriend off at her home on his way. Alfie and I waited a while before we went for our walk due to the sub zero temperatures.

When we did venture out, we called in to see Marion and Wayne. I enjoyed a hot cup of coffee and a warm, by their roaring fire. Alfie wasn't at all keen, the noise of the wood crackling frightened him. Outside there was a thick frost and it was not letting up.

Once we had returned home, I heated some of the leftover asparagus soup, I just needed something hot to warm me through. I felt really chilled. After lunch I did a short meditation then I had to go to Madam President's for a W.I. committee meeting. She gave us a lovely piece of Christmas cake with a cuppa.

Again I was feeling a bit spaced out and decided I really didn't want to take on much this coming year. I think it is time I was kind to myself. I normally put everyone else first but now my head won't let me.

It was getting dark and a lot colder by the time I took Alfie out for his nighttime walk. I was pleased when we were back home. Tonight I had made delicious stewed steak with dumplings, creamed potato and vegetables for Paul and myself, just the ideal supper for a winter's night. Paul had decided to come and stay with me as his girlfriend was working. I was delighted and very grateful.

I love to see him but understand he is only twenty two and his friends and his dad also want to spend time with him when he is home.

Paul sorted out my mini printer which I had bought for myself last year enabling me to print photos off my iPhone. I hadn't used it for a while and had therefore forgotten how to use it. I think it's that thing....getting older! Paul set it up, gave me a quick lesson on how to use it again then I spent the evening printing my photos whilst Paul was watching T.V., I was in my element.

Thursday 29th December

I had to say goodbye to Paul today, he was flying back to Dubai. He had a race on the 2nd January in Al Ain but he had to prepare everything plus I think he had plans for New Year's Eve in Dubai with his friends.

I found it so hard, I had gone into his bedroom to say goodbye but had to make a quick retreat into the bathroom as I couldn't stop the tears. I sat there until I got myself under control then went back in to say my goodbyes.

I was off for my appointment with the chiropractor but there was a hard frost again this morning and I wanted to take my time. Because it was still the Christmas Holidays, I did find the roads a lot quieter. The run down to Sunderland was really enjoyable.

Alfie and I enjoyed our walk along the sea front, this was truly a bonus to our days when we had to make the journey to Sunderland.

But no time for dawdling, yet again, as today I had friends arriving, they were coming for tea and staying over. So when I got back I had the bed to strip and change and also a meal to prepare. We were leaving early in the morning for the Scottish Highlands, where we were going to celebrate the New Year and hopefully it would be a much better year.

I found it strange and quite sad saying goodbye to 2016 because I felt I was saying goodbye to Steven all over again. 2016, the year I lost my darling boy.

The Anniversary

Sunday 6th August 2017

Steven's first anniversary. I had been feeling very tearful and very tired for the past two weeks, last night I got a huge lump in my throat and felt both sickly and panicky. Gill text me and told me to go down to their house in Sunderland and stay over, which I did.

I was going to the church where we had had Steven's funeral and my friend Gill was coming with me today. I was really grateful to her because I felt no more like being on my own.

I was sitting having breakfast at Gill and Roy's when I heard music, it was quite quiet and I had to ask Roy if it was Johnny Cash and he said yes it was, it was the track we had played at Steven's funeral, 'God's Gonna Cut You Down.' Steven was letting me know he was still with me.

I went with Gill to church, I broke down as soon as I walked in the church door. Steven's name was mentioned in the intersessions, Pat was sitting beside me, holding my hand and giving me support, as Gill was doing her Church Warden duties. Having to sit through the service was a lot harder than what I ever imagined it would be.

After the service, I collected my sister Joy and her daughter Kathryn and Kathryn's son Matthew. My sister-in-law Judith followed on behind in her car. We were going to the crematorium to read the entry in the Book of Remembrance then visit Steven's grave.

When I read the passage which the ex had had printed in the book, it didn't even mention the fact that Steven had a mum. So much for him saying he would include me.

Judith, asked if I was not going to write in the visitors book. I told her that there was no need, Steven knew how much I love him and miss him.

I walked out and left Joy and Judith reading the book as I went and sat on the seat which had been put there in memory of my brother Cecil, after he had died.

Judith left shortly afterwards, she had arranged to go out for lunch and the rest of us went to visit Steven's grave.

When I got to the graveside, an additional headstone had been put there, which I had not known anything about. The ex had omitted to tell me and there was also a wreath the size of the gravestone from him and Paul.

I had expected him to do this with regards to the wreath but I was prepared. I had gone on the internet and purchased a vase which would go into the ground, on it had 'In Loving Memory of a Dear Son' and so armed with my vase and a bottle of water, I was able to arrange the beautiful white roses I had bought in Steven's memory.

When I went back to my sister's, she invited me in for a coffee and a bite to eat, which I enjoyed and we chattered about Steven before I returned home to Weardale. Joy said that the entry in the Book of Remembrance was out of order and I said it didn't matter, everything was as it should be and not to worry. It had been quite a morning and I felt quite drained.

Four days before Steven had died, I had attended a Night at the Opera at a local pub, where we dined and listened to seven opera singers. They had sung 'Bring Him Home' from Les Miserables. I had cried all the way through it and in my head I was thinking of Steven.

In hindsight, I think I had had a premonition that I would be bringing Steven home, which indeed I did but not as I would have expected or ever thought.

This year the Night at the Opera was on Steven's anniversary and I knew it was significant, something told me that I would get a message. My friends thought that I would not want to go but I said I had to.

Well I went with four friends. The evening was very upbeat and we were enjoying the food, the singing and the company. Just before the performance ended the singers announced that just that afternoon, they had added one last song to their programme. The song was 'Somewhere Over The Rainbow' I cried. My friends looked at me with knowing tearful eyes, I had received my message.

Heaven lets me know that it doesn't matter where I am, my boy is with me, my heart was singing.

A couple of days later, after much thought about all of the hurt that the ex had caused me, I decided to do a little ritual, once and for all, this was going to end.

I bought three small plants (Pinks) sweet smelling, two were red and one pink in colour and because I don't have a garden, I dug a hole in the soil of my big pot, the one with the dragonfly on the front of it. As I dug, I said a prayer and I thanked my past which I was placing into the hole. I thanked it for the lessons I had learnt, for the people who had been and were no more, for the good times and the not so good, for they had all gone to make me who I am today. I lay them all to rest and on the top of them as I filled the hole in, I planted my three plants. I fed them and watered them and asked God to bless them. (They have never stopped flowering, even through the deep snow in 2018 they were still in flower.)

I will love myself, this person who is one of God's beautiful creations, I will nurture and love her, feed her with nutritional food, take loving care of her, make sure she has plenty of rest, fun and laughter and I will go forward to write another chapter, hopefully many more chapters.

When I did my housework a couple of days later, something told me to put Steven's Book of Remembrance and Plaque away which I had had standing on my fireside hearth. I questioned it but the voice in my head told me to do it, Steven did not want a shrine.

I moved the white roses from beside his photo onto a nearby coffee table and moved both the boys' photos from the hearth onto the mantlepiece, putting them one at either side. My beautiful boys, they have certainly been and always will be a treasured gift from God.

As I did this, I felt a weight being lifted off my shoulders. I was now able to focus on the love I have for both of them and the happy memories but not the grief, which I had been doing over this past year. It was time to get on and live this precious life which God has given me.

I will keep both of my boys safe in my heart, knowing God watches over Paul wherever he may be, keeping him safe at all times. God also surrounds Steven, my brother Cecil, my mum, my dad, my grandparents and my ancestors with His love in Spirit.

How can I accept Steven's death you may ask?

Well when Steven was twenty five he suffered from deep depression and one Friday night, when he was at his lowest, I persuaded him to get help at our local hospital.

Whilst sitting in a side room in A&E, waiting for the Crisis team to arrive. Someone just happened to mention that if they sectioned Steven then he would get the help he needed. As soon as Steven heard what they were planning to do, he up and bolted out of the door. He was off like a shot, no-one was able to catch him. The hospital staff phoned for the police to try and help find him. His dad and my nephew went out looking for him too.

I was left in the room on my one, not knowing what to do. The only thing I could do was pray. I said the 'Miracle Prayer' which a friend had given me a few years before and which I had a copy of, on my mobile phone. I prayed from my heart and said to God that if His needs were greater than mine then I understood but if Steven wasn't meant to die could God please get him the help he needed. I also asked Archangel Michael to protect Steven and Mother Mary to keep him in her care until such time he would come back to me.

The hospital staff advised me to go home, just in case Steven went back there. I arrived home and my neighbour Maria, came to sit with me. She didn't want to leave me on my own and so we curled up on the settees, drinking coffee and just waiting for some news.

Unknown to me, Paul who was away in Scotland racing, had put on Facebook that should anyone see his brother could they let us know.

Well at 2:45 a.m. I received a text from one of Paul's friends to say that he had spotted Steven walking along the beach at Seaburn, heading towards Whitburn and the cliffs. He asked what should he do and I suggested he follow Steven but at a distance so that Steven wasn't aware that he was there. In the meantime I rang the police, gave them Paul's friend's mobile number and eventually with the help of the police helicopter and the policemen on the ground they caught up with Steven on the cliffs at Whitburn.

Steven spent a weekend in a psychiatric ward. I have to say he was very angry on the Saturday morning. He was sending abusive texts to me, which I ignored. By the afternoon the texts changed, Steven was now pleading with me to go and visit him.

I phoned the staff to ask their permission and they allowed me to visit on the Saturday evening and again on the Sunday afternoon. When I went in on the Sunday afternoon and was walking towards Steven's room, I could hear laughter, Steven's laughter!

A nurse called Michael, had talked to Steven for three hours and had turned Steven around. By the Monday, after I attended a meeting of twelve officials, I was allowed to take Steven home for a trial period but we had to go back on the Thursday and report on how he had coped.

I literally had got my boy back. His life improved from that day on. He bought himself a Harley, was offered a job at Harley Davidson, Silverlink, he was happy and he went on to live the happiest days of his life.

So when I got out to Dubai, and was hearing all about what had happened, I just knew it was time for Steven to go back, he had lived his dream and done what he had come to this earth to do. God was calling him home. I accepted his death, I thanked God for taking Steven so quickly and I have never been angry with anyone.

For the last twelve months, I have been having 'One to One' sessions with God as I walked Alfie. I have prayed and given up to God all of my worries.

I couldn't share God with a congregation, that's why I couldn't go to church. I realise that now. I needed it to be just me and God and so as I walked the country paths, sat by the river or waterfall, walked along a deserted beach. I have prayed and talked to God, asking Him to carry me on my very dark days, hold my hand as I started to get on with my life and be there listening when I needed Him to still my mind. He has never not been there for me, I have kept my faith, it has been unwavering.

When I returned after my pilgrimage in 2017, I realised Paul was staying overnight in the same village as I was and so I text to see if it was at all possible for us to meet at the roundabout in the village. It seemed a shame to miss an opportunity to see him, if only for a couple of minutes, to hold him, give him a kiss and have the opportunity to tell him how much I loved him before he went back to Dubai. This we did.

I had sat from 11:30 until 12:20 p.m. He arrived, I got my wish and he went on his way. I knew he was an hour later than what he should have been, to catch his plane back to Dubai. I asked God if He could help.

At 1:15 p.m. I text Paul to ask if he had indeed got to the airport in time. He said he had, check-in had closed but after pleading with the airline staff, they had allowed him to indeed check-in and board the plane. Thank God.

I said yes indeed thank God, my prayers had been answered.

Miracles really do happen but you have to ask first and I think that is what people seem to forget to do, to ask!

This book was mostly written in 2016.

It is my story of events that have taken place in my life.

It had taken me fifteen months to grieve, travel and eventually in October 2017, something told me to visit Bali. Whilst I was there a priest gave me a blessing and purification. During this 'one to one' ceremony I had to offer my grief to the ocean.

I came home and people said I looked different, I was like my old self, I had definitely got my mojo back and it was time to move on with Steven forever in my heart.

And so it is, all is well. Thanks be to God.

Amen.

I dedicate this book to my most precious beautiful boys. Steven in Heaven, until we meet again and to Paul in Dubai, may God watch over you and always keep you safe wherever you are and whatever you are doing. I love you both with all my heart but I miss you both so much more.

May God bless you and thank you for reading my book,
I am truly grateful.

Please watch out for my next book
"The Misfit"
This is Steven's story told through my eyes.

I look forward to reading your comments
please email them to

paulinemessenger@icloud.com

Thank you.

Artwork book cover - jntmelody@gmail.com

Lightning Source UK Ltd.
Milton Keynes UK
UKHW041244300819
348843UK00001B/33/P

9 781788 767354